GET IN THE GAME

Advantage.

Published by Advantage, Charleston, South Carolina.
Member of Advantage Media Group.

ADVANTAGE is a registered trademark, and the Advantage colophon is a trademark of Advantage Media Group, Inc.

The Great Game of Business®, Great Game®, A Stake in the Outcome® and The Great Game of Education® are registered trademarks and Critical Number™, MiniGames™, Know & Teach the Rules™, Follow the Action & Keep Score™ are trademarks of The Great Game of Business, Inc. All rights reserved. Registered and/or pending trademarks of The Great Game of Business in the United States and international countries are used throughout this work. Use of the trademark symbols are limited to one or two prominent trademark uses for each mark.

Printed in the United States of America.

10 9 8 7 6 5 4 3 2 1

ISBN: 978-1-64225-130-2
LCCN: 2019910242

Book design by Jamie Wise.

This publication is designed to provide accurate and authoritative information in regard to the subject matter covered. It is sold with the understanding that the publisher is not engaged in rendering legal, accounting, or other professional services. If legal advice or other expert assistance is required, the services of a competent professional person should be sought.

Advantage Media Group is proud to be a part of the Tree Neutral® program. Tree Neutral offsets the number of trees consumed in the production and printing of this book by taking proactive steps such as planting trees in direct proportion to the number of trees used to print books. To learn more about Tree Neutral, please visit **www.treeneutral.com**.

Advantage Media Group is a publisher of business, self-improvement, and professional development books and online learning. We help entrepreneurs, business leaders, and professionals share their Stories, Passion, and Knowledge to help others Learn & Grow. Do you have a manuscript or book idea that you would like us to consider for publishing? Please visit **advantagefamily.com** or call **1.866.775.1696**.

To my mother, Patty, who will always be my biggest fan. No matter what I do.

To my wife, Alicia, who changed my world. Never been happier.

To my kids, Ryan, Rylee, Ethan, and Jackson, who make it all worth it.

- Rich Armstrong

To my wife, JoAnn, who showed me who I can be.

To my kids, Colin, Madison, and Jackson, who amaze me every day.

To my mother, Glenda, who taught me what being good really means.

And to my dad, Joe…you were right.

- Steve Baker

TABLE OF CONTENTS

FOREWORD vii

PREFACE ix

INTRODUCTION 1
YOU ARE NOT ALONE

STEP 1 26
BEGIN WITH THE RIGHT LEADERSHIP

STEP 2 36
SHARE THE WHY BEFORE THE HOW

STEP 3 44
OPEN THE BOOKS AND TEACH THE NUMBERS

STEP 4 60
FOCUS ON THE CRITICAL NUMBER

STEP 5 82
ACT ON THE RIGHT DRIVERS

STEP 6 88
CREATE AN EARLY WIN WITH MINIGAMES

STEP 7 112
PROVIDE A STAKE IN THE OUTCOME

STEP 8 134
KEEP SCORE

STEP 9 148
FOLLOW THE ACTION— HUDDLES AND FORWARD FORECASTING

STEP 10 180
SUSTAIN WITH HIGH-INVOLVEMENT PLANNING

READY, FIRE, AIM 203

ACKNOWLEDGMENTS 209

ABOUT THE AUTHORS 213

APPENDIX: THE HIGHER LAWS OF BUSINESS 215

FOREWORD

Who would ever have believed that a musician and an art major could become some of the best business resources in America? Rich Armstrong and Steve Baker have become the greatest teachers of The Great Game of Business leadership system. They have earned their PhDs over the countless hours and miles they have invested in learning the power of The Game as practitioners themselves at SRC, as well as helping others implement it across every industry you can think of, from government and healthcare to technology and education.

These guys have worked with people for decades crafting the right messages and developing accelerated learning programs like the one you'll find inside the pages of this book. They are the ones who have ultimately helped drive home the impact that playing The Game can have to a broad audience—which is something I personally have been trying to do for nearly forty years. When Bo Burlingham and I wrote our book *The Great Game of Business*, about our experiences playing The Game inside SRC, I was busy trying to grow a company. It was these guys who picked up the ball and ran with it.

Rich and Steve have been the drivers of this movement, creating a deep history of people and organizations playing The Game. They were the ones who answered the questions that came up and provided information whenever someone wanted it. They not only established the Great Game of Business library—they built an organization, a network of coaches, and a community of practitioners around it.

They wrote this book, *Get in the Game*, because people asked them to. This is their response to what the marketplace demanded. This book is the culmination of all those questions they've been asked over the years, especially the big one: How do you start playing The Game? This book is the answer to that question.

But the thing that really impresses me the most about these guys is that they have a true passion for playing The Game. They believe it's the right thing to do because they have seen the impact that this system can have on so many people's lives. They believe that the American Dream is still alive. And that it's by applying the common sense lessons that come from playing The Game that someone can achieve their own version of that dream. With this book, they are leaving a legacy for generations to come.

—Jack Stack
Co-Founder and CEO, SRC Holdings Corporation and author of *The Great Game of Business*

PREFACE

The Great Game of Business has grown from a curiosity thirty years ago into a significant and profitable leadership system. People often tell us The Game sounds wonderful, but they want to know if it really works. Will it work in a retail business, a *Fortune* 500 company, a union shop, or a nonprofit? The answer is a simple, unqualified yes. Any organization whose performance can be measured with financial statements can play The Game. From one guy working in his basement to multinational corporations, The Game will work anywhere, provided you want it to work.

It's not a system, a philosophy, an attitude, or a methodology. It's all those things and more. It's about tapping into the universal desire to be a winner. We know from experience that the best, most efficient, most profitable way to operate a business is to educate everybody on how the business works, give them a voice in saying how the company is run, and provide them a stake in the financial outcome: good or bad. Constant improvement of your way of life and your livelihood are the payoffs for playing The Game. Play together as a team, reap the rewards, and build a dynamic, competitive company at the same time.

One of the best places to start playing The Game is by reading this book. As you read, ask questions, challenge the process, look for things relevant to you, and focus on the ideas that strike a chord with you and the people you are working with. Then bring those challenges and concerns back to the community of thousands of other companies playing The Game. Start wherever you feel comfortable, and then keep going. Build on your successes. Learn from your mistakes. Don't give up. The Great Game of Business works for everyone who keeps trying to improve the bottom line in business and in life.

—Rich Armstrong and Steve Baker

INTRODUCTION
YOU ARE NOT ALONE

hances are this is not the first business book you've read. In fact, in the United States alone, over one thousand business books are published each month. It's more likely that you've read everything you can get your hands on to figure out why your organization isn't giving you what you want, need, or aspire to. It might even be that you found this book after years of tracking down best practices, implementing them, and wondering why they didn't fix everything.

Well, you are not alone. Entrepreneurs worldwide have followed your same path, with similar results. Your team may even think of you as suffering from "business by best seller." You go to a conference, discover the latest best practice, and then install it in your business when you get back home in hopes of transformation. Only when you do, you get a bunch of eye rolls or lackluster execution. If you've ever looked over your shoulder, wondering why no one was following you, this is the book for you.

The Great Game of Business is the open-book management operating system based on the *only* aspect of business that has been around since the 1400s and the one thing that will never go away: the financials.

IT'S MONEY. IT'S PEOPLE. IT'S BOTH.

You've seen the spectrum in business management systems. On one end of the spectrum are the numbers: cash, metrics, KPIs (key performance indicators), OKRs (objectives and key results). On the other end is culture: systems fostering a great place to work, with shared values and common purpose.

In the middle, though, is truly where the magic lies. The pendulum swings both ways, and too far in either direction can throw you off-kilter. There's a secret "balance" hiding in plain sight. All the business "gurus" have missed it. It's not just financial results; it's not just cultural change. What the experts have missed is that during the entire Industrial Revolution, companies tried to boil business down to quotas and metrics that simpleminded workers could understand. And by doing so, they inadvertently divorced the people who create the numbers from the financial health of the business. They missed tapping a wealth of discretionary energy and talent. It's the reason so many people have felt as if "I was doing my job really well. How did I get laid off?" Or to the other extreme, in a culture of unlimited vacation, nap rooms, and bring-your-dog-to-work days, "This was such a great place to work! Why did we close down?"

The Great Game of Business (GGOB or The Game) is the only business operating system that reconciles this people-profits paradox, balancing the need for profit with the needs of our people. It's finance, *and* it's culture. It's substance, *and* it's soul. It's money. It's people. It's both.

It really is about *both* financial results and a great culture—a combination that in our experience creates successful, sustainable companies.

The Great Game doesn't just build businesses. It builds people.

The Game sets people up for success through education, involvement, and opportunities for rewards—improving not only their financial position but their quality of life as well. The bottom line is this: Great Game companies understand that when employees win, the company wins. And Great Game employees understand that when the company wins, they win. This may be the only management system that consistently moves both the company and its people closer to their full potential—partly because The Game has never been just about generating profits, cash, and wealth but also about using it for the good of the people and their communities.

It's worth repeating: It's money. It's people. It's both.

WHAT IF PEOPLE ACTED LIKE THEY OWNED THE PLACE?

Imagine working in a company where everyone was engaged and acting like they owned the place. Where they were truly excited and energized by the goals of the company and knew how they contributed.

What if all the people working there—not just the owners or managers—truly understood the marketplace, the competitors, and what it really takes to compete and consistently grow the business? What if everyone truly grasped how difficult it is to make money and how most profit never ends up in the owner's wallet?

In short, what if they acted less like employees and more like owners?

Sound impossible? It's not. Companies large and small have run their organizations using The Great Game of Business for nearly forty years and have achieved extraordinary results. We've seen it work in thousands of companies around the world, in every industry—public and private, for-profit and not-for-profit—with amazing results. It may be the only sensible way to run a company.

Let's be clear about what we mean about thinking and acting like an owner. It's not about equity. In fact, 85 percent of the companies who practice The Great Game of Business are not yet sharing equity, but they still see the results. Ownership is a mind-set. Think about the last time you rented a car. Did you treat it differently than the cars you own? Unless you were prepared to check the tire pressure, add wiper fluid, and schedule the preventative maintenance, you can probably relate to the point. We treat things differently when we feel a sense of ownership. It applies to cars, apartments, homes, and yes, businesses. Ask yourself this question: "Do my people act like they own the place, or do they act like they rent it?" Ouch.

When we talk about ownership, we are referring to the mind-set—the behavior and the attitude. If you want employees to think and act like an owner, you must treat employees like owners. You must involve them in the business much like owners are involved. You must ask everyone to understand the business, set goals, make a plan, take responsibility, and even share in the risk. And if they are successful, they should also share in the rewards. That is how you sow the seeds of true engagement and create an ownership culture.

All this starts with getting your people in the same game the owner is: the game of business. It may be the most powerful engagement lever you can pull. You can build a winning culture by creating a business of businesspeople.

Engaged employees take responsibility. They desire to contribute to the success of their team and of the company, and they have an emotional bond with the organization and its mission and vision. In today's labor market, people want to be recognized for their contributions and to be valued as individuals. Meeting an individual's innate need to be individually recognized for a job well done and giving them the opportunity to win as a member of a team improves their levels of satisfaction, involvement, and motivation at work. Allowing employees to contribute to a greater good and valuing their contribution inspires loyalty and commitment. At the end of the day, it's all about creating a winning company and a company of winners.

ORIGINS OF THE GAME

The underlying power of The Great Game of Business is that it's just plain common sense. It wasn't theorized in a business school or dreamed up at some consulting think tank. It was created by everyday businesspeople much like you almost four decades ago at an engine remanufacturing plant in Springfield, Missouri.

In 1983, Jack Stack and twelve other managers scraped together $100,000, borrowed $8.9 million, bought a dying division of International Harvester, and transformed it into what has become SRC Holdings—one of the most successful companies in America. (You can read the full version of that story in *The Great Game of Business*.) But for that evolution to happen, things needed to change—fast.

Stack was amazed that 119 machinists, engineers, and plant workers could be the *absolute best in the world at their jobs* and yet still face layoffs because their company was failing. But Stack learned an incredible lesson when he went on a quest to secure the financing they needed to save the plant and the jobs. As he approached bank after bank (fifty-three turned him down), he discovered that a secret universal language was being spoken in business—one he did not yet know or understand. It was the language of business and the language of owners: the financials. But Stack recognized that if they were going to save jobs, everyone in the company should understand and speak that same language.

He knew that to protect the jobs over a long period of time, they would need to build a company that would be profitable, growing, and sustainable. Stack needed everyone to know that since they were operating with a debt-to-equity ratio of 89:1, they could not afford to make a single thousand-dollar mistake! So together they learned, set a goal, assigned accountability, and showed the risk as well as the reward. What followed were a legendary turnaround and a radical new approach to running a company based on unleashing the untapped potential in every employee. It was considered radical, because back then, teaching employees business and treating them like owners was heretical. It was simply unheard of. In fact, nearly forty years later, some might say it still is.

CREATING A BUSINESS OF BUSINESSPEOPLE

The Great Game of Business is based on a simple, yet powerful belief: *"The best, most efficient, most profitable way to run a business is to educate everybody on how the business works, give them a voice in how the company is run, and provide them a stake in the financial outcome."* The *strategy* of implementing The Great Game of Business operating system is to *build a business of businesspeople who think, act, and feel like owners.*

Taking a look at the big picture, The Great Game of Business is a way of running your company that gets everyone at all levels of the business as informed, involved, and engaged as the owner is in making the company successful. It's about fully engaging employees by teaching them how the business works and what is critical to success. This includes understanding how profitability is driven, how assets are used, how cash is generated, and most importantly, how their day-to-day actions and decisions can make or break the business. The Game is just plain common sense. When you harness the collective wisdom of your people, great things can and do happen, not just to the bottom line but inside the hearts and minds of your people.

The result is long-term success for your company and long-term success for your people. You will improve your business results and the lives of the people who create those results.

The Great Game of Business is the systematic way to get everyone focused on building a better business. It teaches all employees the goals of the company and how they can make a difference, both individually and as part of a team. It works because employees get a chance to take responsibility and ownership of the company's success rather than just "doing their job." Instead, every employee knows enough about the company to understand how their actions affect their personal rewards or their Stake in the Outcome.

BEYOND OPEN-BOOK MANAGEMENT

For nearly forty years, we've been known as the "open-book people." For the record, the term open-book management (OBM) was coined by John Case of *Inc.* magazine back in the 1990s. The name stuck. In fact, Case wrote the groundbreaking book *Open Book Management: The Coming Business Revolution* about companies that practiced OBM like SRC. With SRC's approach to OBM and GGOB's outreach to help others, Jack Stack was dubbed the "Father of Open-Book Management" by *Inc.* But if you ask Jack what he thinks of OBM, he'll tell you—it's not just about opening the books! Financial transparency is worthless without education, accountability, and reward. The only way to see your people *and* your organization grow and transform is to teach employees how business works.

We've learned that the term *open-book management* can mean different things to different people.

When you mention the term *open book* to business owners and CEOs, many of them will respond by saying, "Oh, yeah, we do that." For these companies, it might involve simply posting the annual report on the bulletin board or throwing up some numbers in a PowerPoint presentation.

For others, they might even share top-line sales figures on a monthly or quarterly basis. Others might make their financial statement available online for any employee to peruse. These companies are open-book reporting, essentially saying, "I'm going to share my numbers with you as long as it's too late to do anything about them." Employees might say, "It's not even open-book reporting—it's more like open-book *boring*."

GGOB goes far beyond simply opening up the books. Sharing financial information does not necessarily mean employees understand or realize how their daily actions and decisions affect financial performance or the health of the company. GGOB is not a spectator sport. It's about understanding how the business works, what the employees' role is in it, and how they can take action. Would a sports team rather have fans who just know the score or players who can *change* the score?

Other times, you might get a look of cynical disbelief if you ask someone if they open their books. "My people don't need to know any of that," they might say with a dismissive shake of the head. "They just need to do their job, focus on their KPIs, and the financials will take care of themselves." But will they?

Yet another response might sound something like this: "I just don't trust that my people will understand the numbers." These leaders feel they need to protect their people from the numbers, as if opening the books were like that scene in *Indiana Jones* where they open up the ark and it melts everyone's faces.

But if you're going to play The Great Game of Business, you need to trust that your people really do want to know what makes the business tick. Contrary to conventional thought, people are far more interested in how they can contribute, how they can make a difference, and how they can tell if they are winning or losing.

There is real power to unleash when you help your entire team—not just your accountants—understand how the company makes money and generates cash. And it's just as critical to establish a line of sight that helps connect how the actions and decisions each person makes on a daily basis impact those numbers. It's the fans who know the score, but it's the players who *change* the score.

It's said that the iconic Netflix culture deck has been viewed more than twenty million times. The deck was co-created by Patty McCord, head of HR and key confidant of founder Reed Hastings during the rise of Netflix. In her book, *Powerful: Building a Culture of Freedom and Responsibility*, she credits reading *The Great Game of Business* for inspiring Netflix to adopt transparency and education when it came to the company's financials and strategic goals:

> *I fell in love with being a businessperson, and I didn't want to be a happy-face HR den mother anymore. I also fell in love with explaining very clearly and fully to everyone in the company why we were making the decisions we were, how they could best participate in achieving our goals, and what the obstacles would be.*

McCord says that the first thing every new agent learned when joining the company was how to read the company's profit and loss (P&L) statement—which might seem like a radical policy until you consider that the goal was to get all agents to understand how their interactions with customers directly impacted the company's bottom line.

Patty understood how important it was to educate their people about the business they were in, empower them to use that knowledge to improve the business, and engage them by giving them a Stake in the Outcome.

STILL RADICAL AFTER ALL THESE YEARS

Forty years ago, teaching people business was heresy. Twenty years ago, it was still radical. Today, even though thousands of organizations and millions of employees worldwide practice The Great Game of Business, they are statistically invisible. It's a big world out there. But with changing times, are we reaching a tipping point?

With a NextGen workforce, transparency and access to data are becoming more commonplace—and *expected*. Capitalism itself is being questioned in its traditional forms. An ongoing war for talent means organizations must go beyond ordinary benefits to truly attract, engage, and retain the best people. Leaders have no alternative but to become the employer of choice. Let's face it: in today's ever-challenging business environment, we can't do it alone. The answer to real, lasting business performance is a higher level of business know-how and engagement at all levels of the company. We need everyone's head *and* heart in The Game.

Here's a question: Why is it that we still run businesses the same way we did in the 1800s? Why is command and control our default style of leadership?

After years of studying the best management practices on the planet, Dr. Gary Hamel, author of *The Future of Management*, noticed that while technology has exploded in the past hundred years, management techniques have not really evolved that much. Looking at the most enlightened and innovative businesses in the past few decades, such as Google, W. L. Gore, and Whole Foods, he makes this observation: "Turns out you don't need a lot of top-down discipline when four conditions are met:

1. Front-line employees are responsible for results.

2. Team members have access to real-time performance data.

3. They have decision authority over the key variables that influence performance outcomes.

4. There's a tight coupling between results, compensation, and recognition."

Sounds like an excerpt from the GGOB playbook, right?

Hamel published that in 2007, twenty-four years *after* Jack Stack and SRC were first lauded in the press for these very concepts.

WHY ANOTHER BOOK ON THE GAME?

First of all, the 1992 book *The Great Game of Business* was an unexpected best seller. Jack Stack's story of the SRC turnaround was so radical and inspiring, it has been cited in a hundred other business books and hundreds of scholarly articles. The idea of open-book management made it a foundational text for business leaders everywhere.

In the nearly four decades we've been practicing The Game, we've learned as much from the GGOB community as we've taught. And it's not only open book; it's open source. As an open-source management practice, companies large and small have applied the immutable principles of The Game to their unique businesses, adding their own special style. Some are household names like Southwest Airlines, Whole Foods, and Netflix. Others have innovated and blazed trails through the years. They discovered firsthand that when you harness the collective wisdom of your people, great things can and do happen. It's the practitioners, not just the living lab at SRC, who make sure that it's a process that is constantly evolving, advancing, and improving. *Unlike any other business practice, The Game has been equal parts revolution and evolution.*

Part of the evolution was the creation of SRC's own coaching, training, and consulting firm—The Great Game of Business Inc.— almost thirty years ago. It was born out of the need and demand of the business community. People who wanted to run their companies differently wanted help.

We've learned a lot from implementing GGOB in other businesses over the years. It's these hard-won lessons that form the basis for the chapters ahead. While there is no one "right" way to approach getting in The Game, we have come up with a set of lessons learned from working with hundreds of companies to help organizations get better results more quickly. We've leaned on our community of practitioners as well as our skilled coaches to help streamline this set of lessons based on what we know works. This is no theory. This book is the product of the insights of those working in the trenches, across every industry or company size you can imagine, to best implement The Game. These are the tips, tricks, and hacks that will make your journey more enjoyable and rewarding.

Never forget that you are now a part of something no other business operating system has quite figured out. The GGOB community is all around you. Not only have we hosted an annual conference for nearly thirty years, The Gathering of Games, but our practitioners actively host visitors regularly to showcase their people, their businesses, and their Game. We have yet to meet a practitioner who would not take a call, answer a question, or invite you to a Huddle. All you have to do is ask, and our team will connect you with someone who can give some friendly advice or lend a hand. And now that you're a part of the community, you have a responsibility to engage your people, be wildly successful, and share your experience with the rest of us. We want to hear your story!

WHAT'S IN A NAME?

The name we use for our system, The Great Game of Business (also known as The Great Game, The Game, or GGOB), has caused a lot of head scratching over the years, especially by people who think that it trivializes business by equating it with a game. Business is serious, they say, where people's lives, let alone life savings, are at stake. It's a fair point. We used the word "game" for our system in the first book because we wanted to find a way to make business approachable and less intimidating to our associates working on the shop floor or in the office. We wanted to break down the walls and hype that make business an elite sport for the select few that keep everyone else in the dark and out of the money. We want people to understand business doesn't need to work that way. There is no reason you couldn't have a company where everyone could play and share in the rewards. Then business would truly be "Great."

The aim is not to trivialize business, but to demystify it. Business is a game, after all. It's not an art or a science. It's a competitive undertaking with rules, ways of keeping score, elements of luck and talent, winners and losers. It can be as exciting, as challenging, as interesting, and as fun as any game—provided, that is, you understand the rules and are given a chance to play. The difference is that in business, the stakes are higher—much higher.

—**Jack Stack**, *The Great Game of Business*

PRINCIPLES AND PRACTICES OF THE GAME

To successfully implement a business system like The Great Game of Business, you should first know what it is and why it's important. You must understand its principles and how they interact. Then you can apply the practices that bring The Game to life.

Business is intimidating to the average person. When Jack Stack sought financing to buy SRC back in 1983, he discovered that bankers and venture capitalists had a completely different scorecard than he did. He measured quality, on-time delivery, safety, and warranty rate. They measured debt-to-equity, days-to-cash, and liquidity ratios. He was there to save jobs. They were there to collect interest payments. With every rejection, Stack realized there were two different games going on, and if SRC was to survive, they'd have to learn The Game of business.

But when you ask great technicians to learn a new skill like business, they say, "Nope! I didn't sign up to be an accountant! Just give me the tools, and get the hell out of my way." (This is universal. We've seen the same effect with software engineers, doctors, and pilots.) How do you teach people business and make it understandable, interesting, meaningful, and maybe even a little fun? That's the challenge, and that's where The Game comes in. Jack had to find a way to demystify business. To make it accessible. So, he used the analogy of a game.

After all, business has the same elements as any game. There's a common goal; there are rules, a playing field, a scoreboard, and a reward for winning. What if we could approach our day-to-day business activities with the same state of preparation, the same level of knowledge, the same enthusiasm, and most importantly, the same desire to win as we do with any competitive endeavor we pursue? Ultimately, we want to help our people understand that business didn't need to be any more complicated than a good game of Monopoly—provided that they understand the rules, have a way to follow the action and keep score, and have a Stake in the Outcome. And at any point in The Game, they understand what winning means.

The analogy of a game works, but don't get hung up on it. These are the basic principles of open-book management. You need to make this your own. Call it what you need to in order to make a change in your organization and start getting results.

Tapping into the universal human need to win, GGOB educates your people in the rules of business, rallies them around a common goal, empowers them to see and improve the score, and engages them by giving them a Stake in the Outcome—presenting them with the opportunity to win as a team.

Great Game companies

- educate employees about the business so they begin to think like an owner;

- empower them to use that education to make better business decisions so they act like an owner; and

- engage employees in driving business results by providing them a Stake in the Outcome so they feel like an owner.

Those are the three principles of The Great Game of Business. Each principle brings astounding engagement and results. While our community has been improving, evolving, and adding to the overall GGOB process, these are the non-negotiable prerequisites for success. Through the years, we've seen great innovation and creativity in how practitioners have applied them. The most successful practitioners have adhered to these proven, core tenets of The Game.

Let's look at each of the key practices.

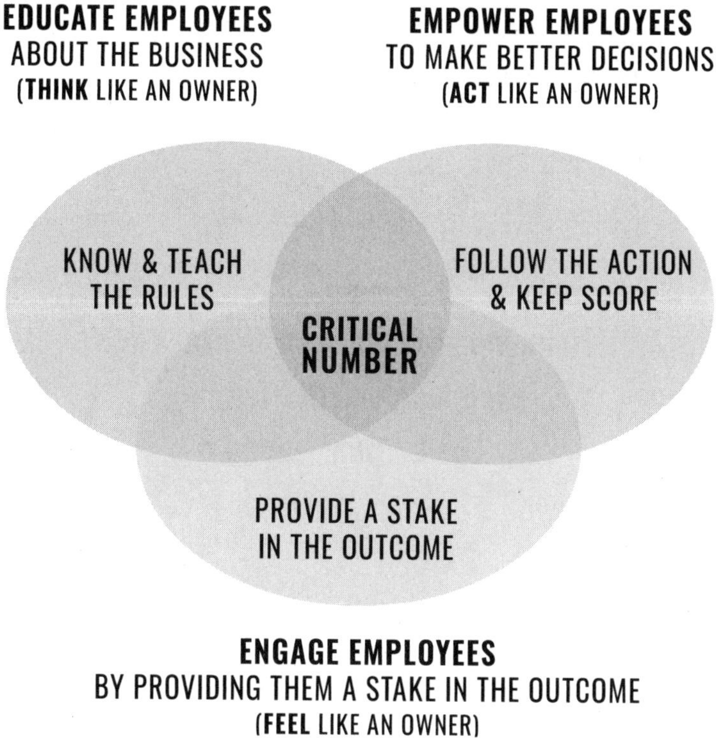

EDUCATE EMPLOYEES
ABOUT THE BUSINESS
(**THINK** LIKE AN OWNER)

EMPOWER EMPLOYEES
TO MAKE BETTER DECISIONS
(**ACT** LIKE AN OWNER)

KNOW & TEACH
THE RULES

FOLLOW THE ACTION
& KEEP SCORE

CRITICAL
NUMBER

PROVIDE A STAKE
IN THE OUTCOME

ENGAGE EMPLOYEES
BY PROVIDING THEM A STAKE IN THE OUTCOME
(**FEEL** LIKE AN OWNER)

Figure 1

KNOW & TEACH THE RULES

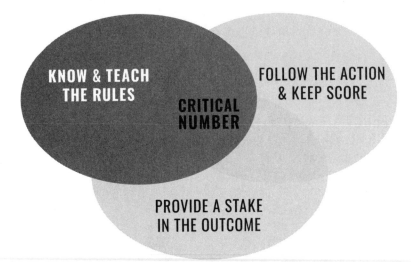

Financial Transparency & Education
High Involvment Planning
The Critical Number

Figure 2

Financial Transparency and Education

The financials are often the only report card in the company that shows the collective contribution of each and every department and individual in the company. So why not use them to bring people together?

If the strategy is to create a business of businesspeople, it follows that employees must learn the language of business—the financials. Nothing can duplicate the informal, practical learning that comes with keeping score and following the real numbers day in, day out. But there is definitely a place for formal financial transparency and training—if it is done right.

High-Involvement Planning

When The Game is created with broad participation—specifically the people who are closest to the action and who understand the realities—it creates a level of commitment and alignment that just can't be matched. High-Involvement Planning helps companies transform their planning process from an annual time-consuming ritual to a highly informative, educational journey that involves everybody at every level of the company in understanding the big picture and the importance of looking forward into the marketplace.

The Critical Number

The Critical Number defines winning. It rallies people around a common goal and a focus on what's most important and critical to the company's success. When the Critical Number is correctly identified, targeted, and tied to a reward, the rules of The Game have been set. The Critical Number becomes the focus of The Game. Once your people know what's critical to success, they must then understand what they can do to drive that success. Identifying the Right Drivers helps everybody begin to understand what they can do, both individually and as a team, to influence the Critical Number and bottom-line financial results.

FOLLOW THE ACTION & KEEP SCORE

KNOW & TEACH
THE RULES

FOLLOW THE ACTION
& KEEP SCORE

CRITICAL
NUMBER

PROVIDE A STAKE
IN THE OUTCOME

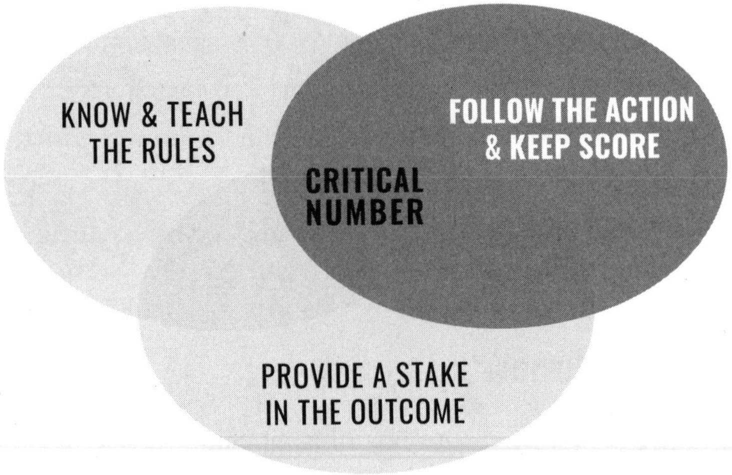

Keep Score - Scoreboards
Follow the Action - Huddles
Forward Forecasting

Figure 3

Keep Score

Winners are fanatics about keeping score. They understand that if you're not keeping score, it's just practice. The primary objective of keeping score is to simply and consistently inform the players if they are winning or losing and who is accountable.

Follow the Action

Following the action through a series of Huddles provides a rhythm of communication where everybody is kept informed, involved, and engaged in the progress of The Game.

Forward Forecasting

You can't change history. Forward forecasting is the fundamental way in which Great Game of Business companies communicate the numbers and create forward-looking, educational, and results-focused Huddles.

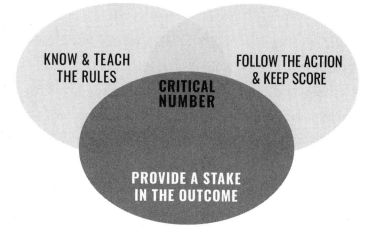

PROVIDE A STAKE
IN THE OUTCOME

KNOW & TEACH
THE RULES

FOLLOW THE ACTION
& KEEP SCORE

CRITICAL
NUMBER

PROVIDE A STAKE
IN THE OUTCOME

Rewards & Recognition
MiniGames
Ownership

Figure 4

Rewards and Recognition

All who directly participate in strengthening the company likely do so because they have some form of a Stake in the Outcome. They come to work to win, because they know their work will result in significant reward, recognition, and ownership in the outcome.

MiniGames

MiniGames are short-term, intensely focused continuous-improvement campaigns designed to affect a change, correct a weakness, or pursue an opportunity within the company. MiniGames are played in work groups or departments to help drive the Critical Number. There is a team goal, a scoreboard, and a reward for winning. It's The Great Game of Business in microcosm.

Ownership

Not all who play The Great Game of Business can or will share equity. Those who do share equity understand that employee ownership doesn't guarantee success. But experience and research have shown that employee-owners have a different attitude about their company, their job, and their responsibilities that increases the likelihood that their company will be successful.

THE TEN STEPS OF IMPLEMENTATION

This book was designed with a focus on implementation. The how-to. The cookbook. The step-by-step approach we use every day to implement and sustain The Great Game of Business inside organizations around the world and in every industry. We designed this book to teach you the principles and practices of the operating system to get you in The Game quickly, tips to make it stick, and methods to start you on the journey of High-Involvement Planning that will help you transform not only your business but your people.

Along the way, you'll find the proven, time-tested tools, case stories, and techniques to successfully implement The Game in your company or organization. In addition to the book, our resource site (www.greatgame.com/gigtools) is incredibly robust and always evolving. Our experienced coaches live and work around the world, ready to help with the challenges you'll face.

1 BEGIN WITH THE RIGHT LEADERSHIP

SHARE THE WHY BEFORE THE HOW **2**

3 OPEN THE BOOKS & TEACH THE NUMBERS

FOCUS ON THE CRITICAL NUMBER **4**

5 ACT ON THE RIGHT DRIVERS

CREATE AN EARLY WIN WITH MINIGAMES **6**

7 PROVIDE A STAKE IN THE OUTCOME

KEEP SCORE **8**

9 FOLLOW THE ACTION

SUSTAIN WITH HIGH-INVOLVEMENT PLANNING **10**

STEP 1

BEGIN WITH THE
RIGHT LEADERSHIP

**If you're not prepared to learn, teach, share and be
involved, The Game will not work for you.**

Is leadership different in an open-book company? Through all of our work with companies implementing the principles of The Game, we have learned quickly that it begins with the right leadership. In other words, critical leadership beliefs and characteristics are present in all great OBM leaders—leadership characteristics that support the leadership system and give it authenticity and momentum. If these characteristics are not present in your leaders of The Game, the system may not reach its full potential and may be at risk of failing.

WARNING: If you have something to hide or want to use the numbers and information to manipulate and control people, find another approach.

If you are not prepared to learn, teach, share, and be involved, The Game will not work for you. However, if you're interested in improving results and the lives of the people who help you drive those results, then The Game might be a great fit for you and your organization.

It's a powerful leadership system, but it isn't for everyone.

The Game is not a quick-fix remedy. Your leadership team must understand and embrace the reality that this is a continuous learning process that requires

- a sincere commitment from leadership, and

- the right leadership approach.

It all begins with a genuine belief in people and in fostering mutual respect and trust. Regardless of how you currently lead, going "open-book" requires you to reflect on not only your style of leadership but also on how you will develop others as your organization grows. Through the years, we've identified core beliefs and characteristics shared by the most successful Great Game leaders.

Great Game leaders believe the following:

- If I don't inform my people, someone else will.

- Given the opportunity, people want to learn the business.

- Provided the education, people can learn the business.

- Given the trust, people will make the right decisions for the business.

- Given the respect, people will contribute to the success of the business.

- People should share in the rewards they help create.

When we work with organizations, we always ask the question, "What characteristics do open-book leaders need to possess?" In all the years of workshops, conferences, and coaching sessions we've facilitated and out of all the traits we've captured, we have found four to be common in leaders that were truly successful in an open-book environment.

Great Game leaders share these characteristics:

- Humility—"I don't have all the answers."

- Vulnerability—"I'm willing to ask for help."

- Servant leadership—"I'm focused on the needs of the team and the company, not my own."

- Courage—"I'm ready to open up and release control."

BEGIN WITH THE RIGHT LEADERSHIP: TASTY CATERING

In 1984, Tom Walter along with his brothers, Larry and Kevin, opened a hot dog stand in Chicago called Tasty Dawg. Over the next five years, the stand grew into a chain before eventually evolving into what it is today: Tasty Catering, a corporate catering service based in Elk Grove, Illinois, which employs some two hundred seasonal workers.

Tasty Catering might be just as well known today for its progressive workplace, which has earned the company numerous awards, including being named multiple times as the psychologically healthiest workplace in America. But it wasn't always so healthy.

From the start, the Walters were hard-charging entrepreneurs who had been drilled in the command-and-control school of management. While the three brothers had created separate roles for themselves in the business—Tom handled sales and finance, Larry operations and logistics, and Kevin payroll and purchasing—there was often overlap

RICH ARMSTRONG & STEVE BAKER

and disagreements that created tension among the staff. Whenever an issue arose, it seemed that all three brothers weighed in with a different solution—which only resulted in confusion and aggravation among the employees.

The more the brothers insisted on weighing in on every decision inside the business, the more they worked—routinely clocking sixty to eighty working hours a week—because they didn't trust that anyone else could do the job as well as they could. That meant they missed many of their kids' basketball and soccer games as well as other important family moments.

Meanwhile, two key employees had become so frustrated with the way the brothers were micromanaging the company that they staged an intervention. They told the brothers that they were sick of being hamstrung and unable to act without first getting permission. If the culture in the workplace didn't change, the pair threatened to quit.

It was a mic-drop moment.

The brothers finally heard the message loud and clear. They needed to let go of the command-and-control ways they had been practicing for thirty years if they ever wanted their people to grow and thrive. "The three of us had to look each other in the face and ask if we could change," says Kevin Walter. "We quickly came to the conclusion that we couldn't afford not to change. We needed a culture that was based on and built around our employees."

The good news was that they had a foundation they could build on. From the beginning, the brothers had shared the company income statement with their employees and built company-wide bonus programs tied to increased sales and a lower cost of goods sold. Now, they needed to further empower those employees by letting them use that information to make their own decisions—while shifting their own roles to become more supportive of their people in the mode of "servant leaders." As a result of the shift on the part of the three brothers, the culture at Tasty Catering made a radical shift, evolving from command and control to a focus on empowering its employees.

That cultural shift also happened to be an essential moment in laying the foundation for Tasty Catering to embrace playing The Great Game as well. When we say, "Start with the right leadership," we're saying that unless an organization's leaders embrace being both humble and vulnerable, The Great Game won't stick. They need to be willing to admit they might not have all the answers. When the Walter brothers changed their management mind-set and their culture, they had primed themselves to embrace The Great Game.

It was a few years later when Tom introduced The Great Game at a Small Giants Community gathering in Germany. It was then that he and his brothers realized what they were missing out on: it wasn't just important to share the numbers; it was also essential to teach their people to think and act like owners.

Then they jumped in with both feet. Larry and Kevin began by attending workshops at Great Game HQ in Springfield and then laying out their implementation game plan—something they put together literally in the back seat of their car as they drove home back to Elk Grove.

"As soon as I finished reading the book, I couldn't wait to get it accepted in our organization," says Kevin. "I was like, 'Wow, this could really work.' The aha moment for me was reading about how we could tie our bonus programs to the balance sheet and not just the P&L like we had done in the past. The Great Game showed us that by teaching financial literacy, we can give our associates a direct line of sight into the business as a whole. It then creates positive peer pressure to be accountable and to do the right thing."

Case in point: Kevin remembers seeing a group of truck drivers question one of their peers who had left his truck idling on a cold winter day. "They asked this guy why he was not just wasting fuel but also putting extra hours on the engine, because they knew what it costs to replace an engine or even a truck," says Kevin.

Another example of The Great Game's impact occurred when Kevin nervously gave up control of purchasing to the kitchen team—something that he thought he was pretty good at. "I took great pride in my negotiating skills," he says. But within the first year of relinquishing that role, he found that the team had shaved another 2 percent from the purchase prices. Similarly, Tom and Larry handed off their day-to-day responsibilities to successors. Strangely enough, the more responsibility the brothers handed off to their people, the better the company performed—and the more engaged their people became in their work.

Embracing The Great Game has also enabled the Walter brothers to cut back on their schedules to the point where they spend more of their time away from the business than in it. (In fact, Kevin made the decision to dedicate himself to becoming a Great Game coach.) The three brothers now trust their employees to run the show—who do it maybe even better than they could. Annual employee turnover has shrunk to about 2 percent in an industry that averages 50 percent, and its profit margins—the highest in company history—are nearly twice the industry average.

"Taking a back seat and letting your employees run the company is the hardest shift to make for many business owners," says Kevin. "But when you can finally admit that you can't do everything and you need people's help, it becomes a two-way street. Your people are ready to step up and help you. Playing The Great Game starts with a sincere belief in people and fostering mutual respect and trust."

• • •

Now that you know more about what it takes to lead in an open-book environment, you might be getting skittish. Why not build a team to help you throughout the implementation process?

DON'T GO IT ALONE ... BUILD A DESIGN TEAM

Experience shows that the most effective way to apply the principles of The Great Game of Business is to simply "get in The Game." As with any game, the best way to learn and improve is to step in and start competing.

People learn by doing, so we recommend you jump right in. Don't just plan, plan, plan, train, train, train—*do* something! If you become paralyzed in the preparation, you may never see the benefits before people get bored, become tired, and give up. We saw a utility company do this in the 1990s, having spent two years in education and training before they ever held a Huddle or played a MiniGame. When you learn any game, the real learning (and improving) comes by jumping in and playing. We suggest you implement The Great Game of Business with the same approach in mind. Think *ready, fire, aim.*

The implementation team, or what we call the Design Team, is charged with literally "designing" the key GGOB practices for an organization. From divining the first Critical Number, to creating the first scoreboard, to designing the initial bonus plan, the Design Team leads the way.

The Design Team is made up of senior management team members, potentially alongside two to three key employee champions. They may include managers, supervisors, or hourly employees who have "it"—a keen understanding of the organization and a desire to see it succeed. Having influencers like this on the Design Team not only gives you insights throughout layers of the company but also street credibility. Later, they will be instrumental in helping form the first "Culture Committees" and other important functions to keep your Game fresh and engaging over the long haul.

The primary role of the Design Team is to become the agent of change within the organization. They will build the awareness of the need for change, create the desire to participate in the change, develop the knowledge and skills to make the change, and provide the reinforcement to sustain the change.

They will also improve their own financial and business literacy so they can help others understand more about the business. They will become the leaders and champions but also the teachers to develop the next level in the organization.

The first assignment of the Design Team is to build awareness and a desire for change by "Sharing the Why before the How."

Download additional resources at www.greatgame.com/gigtools.

1 — BEGIN WITH THE RIGHT LEADERSHIP

SHARE THE WHY BEFORE THE HOW — 2

3 — OPEN THE BOOKS & TEACH THE NUMBERS

FOCUS ON THE CRITICAL NUMBER — 4

5 — ACT ON THE RIGHT DRIVERS

CREATE AN EARLY WIN WITH MINIGAMES — 6

7 — PROVIDE A STAKE IN THE OUTCOME

KEEP SCORE — 8

9 — FOLLOW THE ACTION

SUSTAIN WITH HIGH-INVOLVEMENT PLANNING — 10

STEP 2

SHARE THE WHY BEFORE THE HOW

People get much more excited about the How when they clearly understand the Why.

I mplementing The Game requires change. And change can be difficult. Too often companies jump right into *how* the change will happen rather than first communicating *why* the change is important. Simply put, people get much more excited about the *how* when they clearly understand the *why*.

In order to effectively implement The Game, we need concrete approaches to building awareness and commitment and, most importantly, a desire to actively participate in the process.

These four elements are required for successful implementation:

- Awareness of the *need* for the change (the why)

- Desire to *participate* in the change (the why)

- Knowledge and skills to *make* the change (the how)

- Reinforcement to *sustain* the change (the how)

With these requirements in mind, how can you build awareness and commitment to The Game? Most importantly, how can you build a desire to participate in the process?

First, recognize your own "curse of knowledge." Your level of understanding and enthusiasm is likely different than that of your leadership team and probably miles from that of your frontline folks. The Game is not the first "best practice" you've brought to your team—and it likely won't be your last. To avoid being left alone with your grand plan, why not help them understand why this is important—to you, the company, and them—before asking them to embrace another best practice?

Through the years, we have seen myriad approaches to introducing The Game to employees. We have seen a number of successful practitioners introduce their teams to The Game and to their own personal why. Some of the most memorable have been when members of top leadership share their heartfelt why with the entire team, outlining what brought them to The Game and why it appealed to them. The truth is that the *reasons* for why someone wants to play The Game are far more important than the *delivery*.

We have seen some pretty tough businesspeople get very emotional while sharing their personal why. Business is life. And life is full of emotion. Being vulnerable and authentic unites everyone in a common cause and solicits buy-in at a deep, human level.

SHARE THE WHY BEFORE THE HOW: ANTHONY WILDER DESIGN/BUILD

Anthony Wilder is a full-service, custom architecture, construction, and interior design provider founded by the husband-and-wife team of Anthony and Liz Wilder. The Wilder team has been creating award-winning projects in and around the Washington, DC, metropolitan and tristate area for more than twenty years. The company's vision from its start was "inspiring everyone to build their dreams" by helping customers imagine, design, and build the homes of their dreams.

Back in 2006, the company was setting records in helping their customers' dreams come true as the housing market boomed. Revenues were way up, and the firm had built up a two-year pipeline of backlog work to come. Everything was going great, and as the old saying goes, "Why fix something that isn't broken?"

But that wasn't good enough for the Wilders. While they were proud of the work they were performing for their clients in fulfilling their dreams, the Wilders wondered if they were building the company of their own dreams. Just as importantly, were they building a place where their staff members could say they had the job of their dreams?

"We wondered if we were truly dream builders for everyone," says Liz Wilder. "We wanted a culture where our employees were empowered to do more and be more. Anthony and I also knew we wouldn't live forever, and we wanted the company to continue on long after we were gone. We want the business to contribute to the community and become something that would be part of our legacy."

The Wilders began to search for ways they could transform their company and fulfill the dreams they had for it and their people.

Enter *The Great Game of Business*. After reading the book and hearing Jack Stack speak, the Wilders decided that The Great Game was a way for them to achieve their goals—and they were willing to take some risks to achieve them. That included sharing with their staff the reasons they were going to open up the books to them and ask for their help in building the business.

In time, part of the Wilders' dream was to also share ownership with their staff—to give the people building the company the opportunity to own it—and they saw The Great Game as a way to get everyone to better understand what is meant by thinking and acting like an owner in the business. "Part of my personal mission is to inspire everyone to build their dreams," says Liz Wilder, "and when I empower others, it inspires me. I wanted to teach everyone how we made money and how they contributed to the bottom line."

By sharing the why behind The Great Game with their team, the Wilders got everyone on their team engaged and excited about playing and learning the how. The early returns were extraordinary as revenue soared and the company added staff. The dream was coming true.

And then the recession hit.

Within just a few months of the collapse of the housing market in 2008, sales at Wilder Design essentially dried up—no one was spending money on new homes or renovating existing ones. They, like just about every firm in the housing and construction industries, were dead in the water.

The Wilders were then faced with an impossible decision: they needed to cut costs—deeply. But how? Everyone understood that drastic measures needed to be taken. Everyone in the company could see the facts staring back at them on their scoreboards. What they didn't want to do was lay anyone off. They wanted to weather the storm together without losing anyone. "Trying to decide who to lay off was like trying to decide what finger to cut off," says Liz.

The Wilders ultimately came to the conclusion that they would make painful across-the-board salary reductions rather than lay anyone off.

Employees would be cut back 20 percent, managers 30 percent, and Liz and Anthony 50 percent. Even those drastic cuts would buy the company just three months of runway.

When the day came to announce the decision to the team, Liz was emotional. She knew people on staff had families to feed, houses to pay for, and college tuition bills for their kids. She didn't know how they would react, and her stomach was tied in knots as a result. She thought of the one carpenter on her staff who had seven kids. What was he going to do?

Finally, as she tried to fight back tears, she gave the team the news. She also promised that if they survived the crisis, the company would pay back all that money. The important thing was that no one was going to lose their job. "We will fight this and survive this together," she told the staff.

There was silence.

Until, from the back of the room, a voice piped up: "Liz, twenty percent is nothing." It was the carpenter with the seven children. "So many of my friends have lost their jobs, and I just learned that I get to keep mine."

All of a sudden, the entire mood of the room shifted. After the meeting ended, staff members came up to Liz and offered to cut their pay even more to help their coworkers who they thought needed the money more. They all came together as a family—and survived the recession.

Scratch that: the company more than survived. It kept its team intact while also putting itself in a position to take full advantage when the economy turned around. By 2011, the company brought everyone's salaries back to normal and even provided back pay—along with 5 percent interest—to its entire staff.

"Without The Great Game of Business, I'm not sure we would have navigated the recession as successfully as we did," says Liz Wilder. "We didn't have to rebuild our team because people knew what was going on financially in the business and why we were making the decisions we were. They participated in it because they understood our Critical Number, our scoreboards, and the things that make a company successful."

Today, sales at the company—which continues to teach financial literacy to every employee—are growing 15 percent per year. But thanks to High-Involvement Planning and the wisdom of the team, the company is also expanding into new markets like interior design and home maintenance as a way to diversify and better prepare itself should another recession roll around. Perhaps just as exciting, the company is also now partially owned by its employees, who participated in a stock purchase program the Wilders put in place in 2016.

"I'm super proud of how The Great Game of Business has trickled down to every level of the company," says Wilder. "We're all pulling for the same thing, which has created such a fun and trusting culture. It's a culture focused on doing amazing things instead of the nitpicking that goes on in so many other companies."

When she reflects back on the journey she, her husband, and the company have been on, Liz Wilder remains grateful that they took the risk in beginning to play The Great Game of Business—all because they understood why they wanted to go on that journey in the first place. "Take the risk," says Liz Wilder. "Be brave, be bold, be open minded. Know what motivates you—and get the help you need to achieve it. By doing that, you will make your life and your business extraordinary."

• • •

If you need motivation, read that last paragraph again. Be brave, be bold, be open minded. Know what motivates you—and get the help you need to achieve it … by sharing your why.

What's your story?

Why are you implementing The Great Game of Business? Why will this be good for *you*? For your *people*? For your *company*?

What results do you hope to achieve? Download additional resources at www.greatgame.com/gigtools.

1 BEGIN WITH THE RIGHT LEADERSHIP

2 SHARE THE WHY BEFORE THE HOW

3 OPEN THE BOOKS & TEACH THE NUMBERS

4 FOCUS ON THE CRITICAL NUMBER

5 ACT ON THE RIGHT DRIVERS

6 CREATE AN EARLY WIN WITH MINIGAMES

7 PROVIDE A STAKE IN THE OUTCOME

8 KEEP SCORE

9 FOLLOW THE ACTION

10 SUSTAIN WITH HIGH-INVOLVEMENT PLANNING

OPEN THE BOOKS AND TEACH THE NUMBERS

Take it beyond just sharing numbers, and begin to build trust and mutual respect through transparency and education.

If you approached an employee at your company and asked them, "Who creates the financial numbers in your company?" what would they tell you? In almost every case, they'd tell you the CFO, the accounting department—the "numbers guy." In reality, they themselves are creating the numbers. With every decision they make and every action they take, *they* are creating the financial numbers in the company.

Too often in business, we fail to show the players the big picture—the overall score of The Game. We tend to try to manage from the sidelines, focusing on individual performance and process results. Meanwhile, the employees—who have their hands on the ball and are most likely to change the score—are left wondering, "What's the score?"

Imagine a vice president who entered his team in a Thursday-night bowling league. The VP figured he knew a thing or two about getting the most out of people. He decided he'd run the team the same way he ran the business.

On the night of the first competition, he rigged up his team's alleys with a big black curtain across the end of the lane, concealing the pins. Behind the curtain, he set up lights and a camera. Then he positioned himself behind the bowlers, where he could watch the pins on a monitor.

The first bowler was a little confused by this, but he figured the boss probably knew what he was doing. So, he grabbed a ball, took his steps, and let it fly. The ball rolled down the alley and under the curtain. The bowler heard the sound of pins crashing and falling. He turned around, looked up at the VP, and asked, "How'd I do?"

The VP peered into his monitor and frowned. "Aim a little more to the left."

The bowler rolled his second ball and heard nothing. The VP's frown turned into a scowl. "Too far, you idiot!" he yelled. It went like that all night long.

By the end of the evening, the VP's team was more than ready to go. This was too much like work. The first bowler, however, still eager to please, asked one more time how he'd done. The VP was shutting off his monitor and gathering up the equipment. "Don't worry about it," he said. "I'll let you know in six months at your performance review."

"But wait!" the other bowlers chimed in. "How did we all do? What was the score?"

The VP glared. "That's really a question for executive management to worry about," he said. "Besides, we won't really know until the end of the season, when the scorekeepers tally up the totals." The VP walked away down the hall, lonely with the weight of responsibility. He muttered under his breath, "What *was* the score?"

Under this scenario, the people who have their hands on the ball and the greatest opportunity to change the score and win The Game have no idea where to take aim. In business, we often forget that the curtain in front of the pins is the barrier. Remove it, and let the players figure out how to change the score—and win The Game.

Although this story clearly explains the benefit of opening the books and showing your people the real score of The Game, there is still a fear from many business owners about opening it up. A real fear—and as a business leader, you need to get comfortable with opening things up.

To begin, let's address the elephant in the room.

GETTING COMFORTABLE WITH OPENING THE BOOKS

Here are the most common concerns people have about opening their books:

Q: What if people see my numbers and figure out how much I make?

A: Opening your books does not mean sharing every detail. Great Game companies rarely, if ever, share salary information. It's divisive. It's distracting. It doesn't help you teach people business. And frankly, they already think you're making more than you are.

Q: What if people see how much the company is making and want more?

A: They already want more. In fact, you want more, too. Everyone does, and you want them to. You want your team to be ambitious, hungry, and wanting more. That's how you'll grow and be sustainable over the long haul.

Q: What if the numbers are bad? Won't people run for the hills?

A: Look, most people (if given the chance) will ask, "What can I do to help?" Opening the books may be the first time in their lives they are treated like adults. Given the facts, people are much better equipped and far more likely to be able to deal with difficult situations.

OPEN THE BOOKS: OUTBACK STEAKHOUSE

When Chris Sullivan and three friends decided to open a new restaurant in their hometown of Tampa, Florida, in March 1988, they wanted to do things differently.

Sullivan wanted to create a business that would give him and his employees the flexibility to enjoy the beaches and golf courses in Tampa. He wanted to experiment with innovative ideas, like opening only for dinner and pruning down the menu to just fifteen items or so from the fifty or sixty items a traditional restaurant might offer. He also wanted to offer premier customer service by having servers cater just eight or ten customers instead of twenty, like they would in most other eating establishments.

But Sullivan had been in the industry for a long time. He had worked in enough restaurants to know that they suffer from a catastrophically high failure rate, mostly because their profit margin is so low. It's really hard to make money in the food business.

He wondered how he could change that in his restaurant. He tried to answer that question by holding a meeting with all the newly hired employees of the restaurant—which they were calling Outback Steakhouse. Everyone from the managers to the servers and cooks gathered together to talk about the kind of business Sullivan envisioned.

He started the conversation with a question to the group: How much money does a typical restaurant make on every dollar of sales? That led to a lively back-and-forth in which a whole range of numbers was thrown around. "Fifty cents! Thirty cents! Seventy cents!" Finally, Sullivan revealed the answer: the typical restaurant made just three cents for every dollar it brought in.

As he said this, a loud laugh came from the back of the room. It was one of the new cooks, who said, "Chris, you do all of this crap for just three cents on a dollar?"

Sullivan smiled. He explained that he didn't want to make three cents; he wanted to make more—much more. He was convinced that the industry was leaving a lot on the table. But he needed everyone's help to get there. In return, he would open up the real numbers about what the business was making and share the extra profits with the employees.

What happened next? Nobody ran away. Nobody quit or complained. Rather, Sullivan's employees stepped up to help. They changed their behavior when it came to watching waste and expenses. They offered exceptional customer service. They owned it and began to make money. Outback's profit margin topped 20 percent, which was shared with employees through a bonus plan.

Those profits also helped the business grow—fast. Eventually, Outback Steakhouse expanded to become a premier restaurant with locations nationwide.

• • •

HOW TO OPEN THE BOOKS: BRIDGE THE GAP BETWEEN PERCEPTION AND REALITY

Do your people know how hard it is to make money? Or have you tried to protect them from the harsh truth?

Why not bring the marketplace—and reality—to your people?

Imagine what people assume about you based upon the car you drive or the neighborhood in which you live. It's amazing what kinds of stories we're capable of dreaming up about the massive wealth the owners of a business are pulling in. Let's focus on one tried-and-true method: teach your people just how hard it is to make money.

When you do that, you can stop the rumors and change the narrative by opening your books and teaching your people how much money your business really makes. If you don't believe us, try it with your people. Turn it into a game, maybe with a prize for who comes closest to answering the question, How much money do we make in profit from every dollar of sales we generate?

Over the past few years, Walmart has averaged about 2.4 cents on every dollar of sales. SRC, the parent company of The Great Game of Business, makes around 5.0 cents on the dollar during a really good year of remanufacturing. In fact, research shows (see figure 5) that the median bottom line among companies in 212 industries across the US is just 6.5 cents. Holy cow! Why get up in the morning?

But how much does the average employee think their company makes? The answer: 36 cents.

PROFIT: PUBLIC OPINION VS ACTUAL

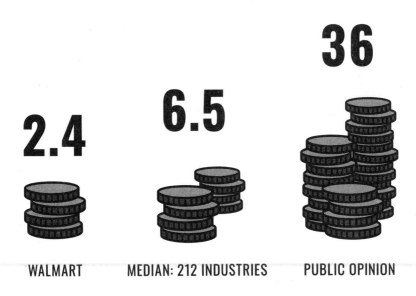

2.4	6.5	36
WALMART	MEDIAN: 212 INDUSTRIES	PUBLIC OPINION

Figure 5

How about *that* for a gap between perception and reality? That is a six times gap in awareness between what companies really make and what their employees think they make.

What kind of decisions are they making under the assumption that you're making six times the profit you really are? If "open book" is scary to you, then "closed book" should be downright terrifying.

The reason this knowledge gap exists is that people are coming to work every day without any information. And so they fill the vacuum with rumors, misinformation, and the most outlandish stories they can think of.

The single greatest argument for open-book management may be that if you don't inform your people, somebody else will.

The good news is that you can stop the rumors and change the narrative by opening your books and teaching your people how much money your business really makes—and how hard it truly is to do so.

THE DOLLAR EXERCISE

Once you show your team how hard it is to make money, they'll see business is a game of pennies. Get your people together, and grab a flip chart.

Grab a flip chart, and sketch out a simplified income statement for your business (see figure 6). Begin by writing out your main "buckets" of revenue. It could be by customer, division, or product line. Next, indicate the cost of goods (COGS). Then, explain how revenue minus COGS equals gross profit (and when expressed as a percentage, gross margin). We love asking the question, "So, are we done spending money yet?" The answer is always "No!" People know that there are expenses: salaries, rent, sales, marketing, and so on.

At the end, we take gross profit minus expenses, and we get net—net profit; operating income; profit before tax; earnings before interest, tax, depreciation, and amortization … what do you consider bottom line? Whatever it is, that is what you should teach your people. This is where you start to teach the language of business—the financials.

Draw a one-dollar bill on the left. This represents one dollar of hard-earned revenue. Ask who knows how much we keep, bottom line, out of every dollar.

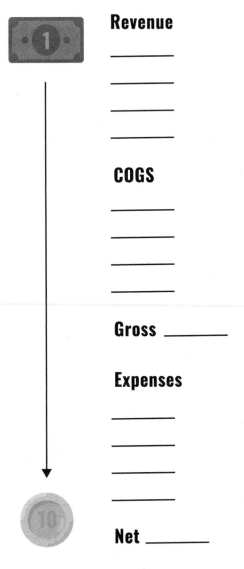

Figure 6

Keep in mind that your people will guess from zero to seventy-five cents on the dollar! Let's say your organization makes ten cents on the bottom line. When you first expose people to the facts, remember the reaction Chris Sullivan got. "Why do you get up in the morning?" could be a response you get from people.

Now you have a perfect opportunity *to bring the marketplace to your people*. Talk about what other companies like yours are doing. Some are *losing* money. Others may be making more than you. Do your homework, and find out what your competition and industry peers are doing. If you have no idea, go try to borrow an outrageous sum of money like we did at SRC. Your banker will share what low, mid-, and high performers in your industry are doing!

If they know the facts and how they stack up against the competition, the average person will respond to your appeal to move the needle, even if only for a few pennies on the dollar. They'll ask, "I had no idea. What can I do to help?"

For the sake of argument, let's ask a simple question: "Would you like to make more money by the end of this year?" We have yet to meet anyone who has answered no. So, if a Critical Number of net profit is okay with you, let's proceed.

With a Critical Number of 10 percent net profit, ask how many dollars we have to sell to get a dollar on the bottom line. Then wait— perhaps for an uncomfortably long time. Your people need to do the math. Eventually, they will calculate that we have to have ten dollars in revenue just to make a dollar in net profit.

> *Coach's tip: To calculate your own revenue number, take one divided by your bottom-line profit number. For example, if you make a nickel in profit, then*
>
> $$1.00 / 0.05 = \$20.$$
>
> *In other words, you must sell twenty dollars in revenue to make that dollar of net profit.*

So, it's clear that to make more money, whoever is responsible for sales better get off their butts and sell! We need a ton of revenue around here! Unfortunately, you'll only engage a small percentage of your team, and the sales team is constantly being pushed to sell more anyway. So how do you engage everyone else, including cost centers like HR, accounting, marketing, and other departments?

We're trying to make people business literate and financially literate. We're trying to build a business of businesspeople, right? What a fantastic opportunity to connect people and give them a line of sight between what they do each day and the profitability of the business.

Draw a dollar on the right side of the simple income statement. This represents a dollar in COGS or expenses. If we don't spend this dollar, does it become a dime on the bottom line? Nope. If we didn't spend it, it's still a dollar … and it drops directly to the bottom line (see figure 7). And in this example, that means every dollar we save in COGS or expenses is worth ten dollars in revenue. Wow.

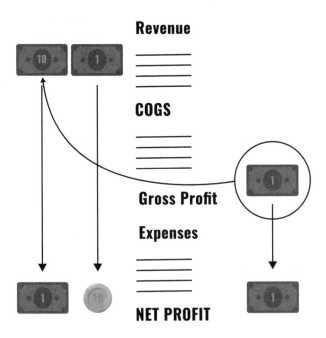

Figure 7

When you tackle this exercise, you've taken your first step toward creating a line of sight for anyone in your organization to see that they can make a dramatic impact. NOTE: The Great Game of Business is not about cost cutting! But teaching a simple income statement is a great place to start teaching people business, isn't it?

You've introduced them to your financial statements. You've also changed their perceptions about how hard it can be for a business to make money while appealing to them to help make a difference. What a phenomenal way to have people begin taking line-item ownership as well.

In time, people will ask why a line is this much, or if they can see the detail behind a number. That's good. Keep teaching them; it will feed your people's appetite to know more.

TEACH THE NUMBERS: FORMAL VERSUS INFORMAL TRAINING

In many companies, if you mention the words *financial literacy*, employees immediately get the shakes. Unfortunately, many companies' training programs don't help matters much. The accounting manager lectures employees in often long, information-overloaded classes, as if the employees are cramming for a chartered professional accountant (CPA) exam.

Sound familiar? It doesn't have to be this way. In fact, teaching and learning business and the financials can be interesting and maybe even a little fun.

The plant manager of a furniture manufacturer kept urging his employees to lower their scrap rates. He deluged them with numbers: cost of materials, production efficiency, and so on. But they just didn't get it. Finally, he called his employees to the loading dock. When they got there, they saw their boss—in front of an old couch with a chainsaw in his hand. Dumbfounded, they watched their boss fire up the chainsaw and lop off about a third of the couch. "That," yelled the boss over the noise of the chainsaw, "is the cost of materials that actually go into our product line." Then he lopped off another third. "And that is our labor cost!" Lastly, he shut off the saw and pointed to the remaining third. By now, you could hear a pin drop. "That," he said, "is how much we're wasting in scrap." He pretty well had their attention by that point.

If the strategy is to create a business of businesspeople, it follows that employees must learn the language of business—the financials. But nothing can duplicate the informal, practical learning that comes with keeping score and following the real numbers day in and day out.

How did *you* learn the numbers? Many seasoned managers understand their numbers not because they went to business school but because they use the numbers every day. Employees will learn the basics of business no differently. If they get an opportunity to see and use the numbers regularly, they'll remember them and begin to understand them. That's why you can't separate financial literacy training from the other parts of your management system, such as frequently tracking and communicating the company's real numbers.

Be sure to support your formal training with informal practices. In other words, use The Game to teach people the business. Remember, you're trying to educate people about your business, not create a bunch of CPAs. Make the learning events casual, interactive, and impactful to them. Continue to put things in context for people, and then reinforce the lessons in frequent engagements around the real numbers.

Ultimately, you want your business literacy efforts to become just another part of your everyday culture.

Our recommendation is that you get the basic practices of The Game in place first, including the informal financial literacy that happens in the weekly Huddles. Then you can build on that foundation with more formalized training. Employees who take that training will come out of the formal classes ready to apply the learning, because they've been living with the numbers for a while.

The point is that a successful financial literacy program is not a one-off event or even something you do every month. If you want to make it stick, it needs to become part of your everyday rhythm and routine, where your people get to learn and apply that new knowledge daily though Great Game practices like Huddles, MiniGames, and updating the scorecard.

When you are ready, establish a formal financial and business literacy training program, but keep the focus on the numbers that matter most to your company, not those that appear in an Accounting 101 textbook. Your people rarely need to know about debits and credits or how to do an adjusting entry. But they may very well need to know exactly how production efficiency is calculated, why receivable days matter, or how the purchase of a new computer system will affect the income statement and balance sheet. The bottom line is that people remember what they find relevant and useful.

In SRC's early days, the employees created a formal class called the Yo-Yo Company, a financial literacy program based on a little boy making yo-yos. It was so simple and approachable that everyone learned the financials without intimidation and could then apply what they learned on the job. Nearly forty years later, we still call it Yo-Yo Company. The financials simply don't change.

The purpose of financial literacy training is to give everyone in the company a common language and boost their confidence in understanding the financial numbers. Then and only then will they begin to make a connection to the numbers that measure their performance, talk intelligently about improvements, and make better, more informed decisions. You'll begin to truly recognize that you have arrived at a business of businesspeople.

BRINGING IT HOME

But the impact of teaching your people financial literacy doesn't stop at the walls of your business.

We've heard time and time again about how the ripple effect of teaching people financial literacy at work results in their bringing those skills back home with them.

That even includes some business owners. Entrepreneur Jeff Evenson created his own financial literacy program for his three kids. Taking it to the extreme, he used $14,000 in real one-dollar bills to show the kids what they spent every month out of the family income, which included everything from the mortgage, taxes, cable, and electricity bills to the various fees and equipment they spent every month on dance classes and soccer and club volleyball fees.

How courageous is this? But doing this exercise can be powerful in helping anyone understand what things cost—especially now that we live in an era where everything just gets charged with a click, tap, or swipe. There is something truly memorable about holding something tangible like a one-dollar bill and giving it away to someone else. Man, you can actually "feel" *that* transaction!

Download the Dollar Exercise and other resources at www.greatgame.com/gigtools

1 BEGIN WITH THE RIGHT LEADERSHIP

2 SHARE THE WHY BEFORE THE HOW

3 OPEN THE BOOKS & TEACH THE NUMBERS

FOCUS ON THE CRITICAL NUMBER 4

5 ACT ON THE RIGHT DRIVERS

6 CREATE AN EARLY WIN WITH MINIGAMES

7 PROVIDE A STAKE IN THE OUTCOME

8 KEEP SCORE

9 FOLLOW THE ACTION

10 SUSTAIN WITH HIGH-INVOLVEMENT PLANNING

STEP 4

FOCUS ON THE CRITICAL NUMBER

Define the win—and get clarity on what's most important and critical to success.

The original Critical Number for Jack Stack and the people of SRC was obvious.

With a debt to equity ratio of 89:1, they needed to make the bank loan payment. If they didn't do that, nothing else mattered—their jobs would be gone. Debt was their weakness, and they needed to drive it out of their business.

Jack used that one common goal to rally people, get their buy-in, and educate them—not only on why it was critical but on how *they* could influence it. Armed with a common goal people could understand and buy in to, Jack could teach debt to equity along with all the related financial education in their weekly Huddles. And after a year and fifty-two lessons, you can be sure they learned it.

THE CRITICAL NUMBER IS AT THE HEART OF THE GAME

Right now, there is at least one financial or operational number in your company, something right at the heart of your business, that if improved in the short term would have a dramatic effect on your business. Does every single person in your organization understand how important that number is?

The Critical Number defines winning. It rallies people around a common goal and provides a focus on what's most important and critical to the company's success. When the Critical Number is correctly identified, targeted, and tied to a reward, the rules of The Game have been set. The Critical Number becomes the focus of The Game.

Our classic definition of the Critical Number is "an operational or financial number that represents a weakness or vulnerability that if not addressed and corrected will negatively impact the overall performance and long-term security of the business."

Think of it as your "one thing"—the one thing that at any given time is going to have the greatest impact on your business. The one thing you must improve to succeed and that clearly defines winning!

In this chapter, we will provide a specific process and tool kit to identify and rally your team around the Critical Number. But before we jump into the process, we need to first share with you a few important ideas that many people miss and that often make all the difference.

YOUR CRITICAL NUMBER WILL EVOLVE WITH YOUR BUSINESS

Your business is in constant change. Therefore, your Critical Number should change with it. The right number for your business could depend on many different factors related to current financial issues, market conditions, operational challenges, and growth goals. That means that your business might need to choose a new Critical Number each year.

At SRC, we often have two Critical Numbers. One relates to profitability, and the other is strategic. It changes from year to year, depending on the particular weakness we see in the company.

FOCUS ON THE CRITICAL NUMBER: REGEN TECHNOLOGIES

A great illustration of how a business put this philosophy into practice is ReGen Technologies, a joint venture formed between SRC and John Deere in 1998. The idea behind the company was for SRC to teach John Deere how to remanufacture the parts it sold through its dealerships. When Ron Guinn joined the firm as president in 2001, however, the company had run into tough times. "It was bleeding money on what should have been a cash cow," says Guinn, now an executive VP at SRC.

Year One Critical Number: Earnings

One of the first challenges Guinn took on with his team was to establish a Critical Number for the business that everyone could focus on and pay a gain share bonus plan on. "My staff of managers and supervisors was highly involved in discussing what our biggest weakness was, how we could get stronger, and how we could create a bonus plan around that," says Guinn. "We'd have meetings where we would come up with ideas and then kick the tires on them for a while as we debated the pros and cons of each. Part of our focus was that we didn't want to pay the partners in the joint venture less than our plans said we would."

In this case, since the business wasn't returning the earnings to the partners in the joint venture they expected, the team first focused on earnings, or profits. "The team needed to get back to basics," says Guinn, "and the P&L was the right place to start."

By basing the Critical Number on earnings, the entire company refocused on understanding what its costs were and how it could work on making processes more efficient. "People responded well by trimming costs and focusing on growing sales through our direct-ship program," says Guinn.

Year Two Critical Number: Earnings and Return on Assets

While many companies choose to keep their Critical Number on profits on an ongoing basis, Guinn understood that if the company is already earning at a top level, you could actually create a disincentive for your team members by linking their bonus to increased profits. "It might be impossible," says Guinn, "which is why it's important to focus instead on whatever weakness you can address."

After some discussion, Guinn and his team realized that the business was loaded with assets, especially inventory. Part of that was because John Deere has a reputation that when a customer wants a part or an engine for a tractor, it will be shipped out the same day.

As a way to better respond to those requests, the company had built up an impressive inventory—but it wasn't always earning the needed cash if it was sitting on a shelf. So, for that year, the team chose return on assets, or ROA, as its Critical Number. That meant the team was focused on turning the inventory—shipping out more of those assets that had been in the warehouse and turning them into cash, which it addressed by playing a series of MiniGames. Ultimately, the improvements the team made in turning around the assets funded its bonus program.

The catch, of course, was that the more the team turned the inventory, the greater the odds it wouldn't have a part on hand a customer might need. "We had to walk a tightrope," says Guinn. "We couldn't draw too much of our inventory down where we might disappoint a customer."

Year Three Critical Number: Earnings and Sales per Employee

Once ReGen had turned its management of assets from a weakness into a strength, the team turned its focus to further improving the efficiency of its operations. Specifically, overhead—especially head count—had started to creep up inside the business. At one point, there were more support people than production people working in the business. The team then decided that everyone in the business needed to add value. So, it chose sales per employee as the next Critical Number. That meant that if a department or a team wanted to add any new people, it had to justify that the new hire would lead to additional sales.

At the same time, Guinn and his team didn't want to grow the top line at the expense of the bottom line. So, they added a second Critical Number—earnings—as a kind of gate. In other words, the company needed to first hit its earnings goals for the year while also hitting its sales-per-employee target in order to earn a full bonus.

A remarkable footnote to the ReGen story is that from 2004,

when they set that Critical Number on sales per employee, and 2008, when John Deere bought the company, the business added only two employees who didn't have a direct impact on sales. By 2008, it had flipped the equation to where it had 1.5 production workers for every support person—and hourly employees were earning up to an extra 18 percent of their annual wages as a bonus.

"Everything we did was designed to make the company better," says Guinn, "and it was amazing that the team hit every Critical Number and maxed out every bonus we threw at them, which taught us to be careful about what you set the bonus on, because people will go after it."

Year Four Critical Number: Earnings and On-Time Delivery

Since the business had begun to excel at maximizing its efficiencies and getting the most from its assets, the team decided that its biggest weakness was on-time delivery.

What the team realized was that there was significant lag time between when an order was placed with the call center and when the order finally made it to the production line. That meant that if the IT and engineering teams could find a way to route those orders more quickly to the production line, they could get the products ready faster to be shipped out without having to stock more inventory.

At the same time, the team recognized that while it had been measuring how quickly it shipped a product or part out the door, it hadn't been tracking when that delivery actually reached the customer's dock. "When we finally started tracking what was most important to the customer, we drastically improved our on-time delivery times by 60 percent in the first year," says Guinn. That improvement also funded the bonus plan, since happier customers would drive more sales—which would then drive earnings based on all the other improvements the team had already made in running the business.

Year Five Critical Number: Earnings and Net Promoter Score

The team took its focus on the customer to yet another level the following year when it set its Critical Number on net promoter score, which is a measure of how willing a customer is to recommend you to a friend or other business on a scale of one to ten. ReGen was an early adopter of net promoter score and hired a third-party company to survey its customers.

"Our focus was to figure out what was most important to the customer," says Guinn. "The assumption was that if we figured out what that was, we could then generate more sales and grow quicker."

ReGen is an unbelievable success story. From 2001 until 2008, when John Deere exercised its option to buy the business, the company grew its top line from $28 million in sales to $100 million. And finding the right Critical Numbers along the way played a huge role in that growth. "I'd love to say that I had a master plan," says Guinn, "but we were just focusing on one thing at a time before we moved on to the next most critical thing. It was quite a ride."

• • •

One lesson you can take away from ReGen Technology's experience is that you will probably start with a profitability-based Critical Number and, with time, evolve by adding a strategically based Critical Number. Successful Critical Numbers like Jack's in those early days of SRC or Ron's at ReGen accomplish three things:

- It focuses a team on what's critical to success.

- It rallies a team around a common goal.

- It educates a team on what they can do to make a difference.

The Myth and Magic of the Critical Number

Myth and magic surrounds the Critical Number. Let's say that you discovered the *ultimate* Critical Number. You found a financial measure that would indicate success—and you're going to focus your entire organization on your ultimate Critical Number and take over the world!

Sounds good, right? But you may be *dead* right. You're right in the sense that *you* have identified the ultimate Critical Number, but you're also dead—dead because you have no buy-in from those who have to execute on it. It's *your* number.

You will continue to hear throughout this book a repeated mantra: *people support what they help create.* When people participate, they buy in. When people buy in, they commit. When people commit, they deliver. That creates ownership in the results—and it's why selecting your company's Critical Number should be a team effort.

It's not a panacea; it's not a magic pill; it's not just about the number itself—it's *how* you get to the Critical Number that matters. And *that* is where the *magic* lies.

PATH TO CRITICAL NUMBER

Long-term GGOB players identify their Critical Numbers as part of the High-Involvement Planning (HIP) process. During the HIP process, strategic and financial plans are developed and scrutinized with broad-based participation in order to identify the Critical Number. (We will share more about the HIP process later in chapter 10.)

For first-time players of The Game, Critical Numbers can be identified through a straightforward business review process, which helps the company get clarity on the realities of the business from four specific areas: financial, marketplace (customer), operational (process), and people (culture). Each area provides a different perspective of the business, and the information gathered is used to identify the Critical Number.

Get your Design Team together to gather data, organize data, prioritize issues, and summarize the issues. Here's a breakdown:

1. Gather data:

   a. Practice assessment

   b. Input survey

   c. Financial analysis template

   d. Benchmarking data

2. Organize data by the four "views":

   a. Financial

   b. Marketplace

   c. Operations

   d. People

3. Prioritize issues in each of the four views.

4. Summarize issues on the Line of Sight Tool (figure 8).

LINE OF SIGHT TOOL

FINANCIAL (NUMBERS) PERSPECTIVE

Things to consider - profit, cash, return, growth, and capital-ization. Sources of information - historical financial state-ments, past financial goals, industry benchmarks and financial trends, internal and external.

MARKETPLACE (CUSTOMER) PERSPECTIVE

Things to consider – market growth/share, value proposition, target customers, and go-to-market strategy. Sources of information – customer surveys, sales & marketing plans, competitive/benchmarking data, market growth, and customer and marketing intelligence.

OPERATIONAL (PROCESS) PERSPECTIVE

Things to consider – capacity, quality, R&D, and cost struc-ture. Sources of information – Practice Scorecard & Input Survey, management interviews, management surveys, and output from operational planning meetings.

PEOPLE (CULTURE) PERSPECTIVE

Things to consider – leadership development, teamwork, and employee engagement. Sources of information – Practice Scorecard & Input Survey, employee interviews, and output from operational planning meetings.

Figure 8

Begin to build your Line of Sight Tool (figure 8) from its foundation, your people, and work your way up.

Your People

Who knows the realities of the business better than the people who are closest to the action? If you are going to ask your people to think and act like owners, you must first *treat* them like owners and ask them for their input. Bring your people together, talk to them, and get to the root of their issues and concerns. This is your first opportunity to engage your people in the process—not only for their input but also for their buy-in and ownership in the outcome. When the Critical Number is identified with broad participation—specifically those closest to the action—it creates a level of ownership, buy-in, and alignment that just can't be matched. When people weigh in, they buy in.

An easy way to get started is with employee and management interviews and surveys. The survey we have used at SRC for over thirty years consists of two parts. The first part is what we call the practice assessment. The Great Game of Business and open-book management isn't about theory—it's about practice. The practice assessment is a complete evaluation of the company's *management operating system* against each of the three principles and nine core practices of The Great Game of Business, identifying strengths and weaknesses.

This assessment also includes an organizational engagement survey to measure overall employee engagement and leadership's commitment to the practices of The Great Game of Business. The practice assessment becomes an essential benchmark tool for companies beginning to practice or already practicing The Great Game.

The second part of the survey contains open-ended questions that help us understand what your people (both management and employees) believe are the critical issues facing the company. We also highly encourage face-to-face talks (interviews) with your people, when possible. Here is a sample of the questions we use:

- What *does* the company do well?

- What *doesn't* the company do well?

- What are the critical financial issues facing the company in the next six to twelve months?

- What are the critical marketplace or customer issues facing the company in the next six to twelve months?

- What are the critical operational or process issues facing the company in the next six to twelve months?

- What are the critical people or cultural issues facing the company in the next six to twelve months?

- What can the company do better, differently, or more of?

- What is one thing we can achieve in the next six to twelve months that would have the greatest impact on the overall performance of the business?

Your Operations

Your operational realities should come through loud and clear in the surveys and interviews with your people. For many of your people, this is the area they know best. They live the operational realities. You will also be able to gain insights from operational benchmarks you collect from your marketplace.

Your Marketplace

We are big believers in bringing the marketplace to our people. Knowing our marketplace helps us clearly define what winning truly means. One of the easiest and quickest ways to explore the marketplace is with the help of benchmarks.

Industry benchmarks are a great way to see how you match up to your industry peers and competitors. It's important that you know what the best of the best looks like and how you stack up against them. Benchmarks can help you quickly identify strengths and weaknesses within your financials and operations. By comparing to benchmarks, you show your people what's possible and create that external competitive spirit we are all looking for.

The best industry benchmarks will come from industry associations. This data is typically captured directly from your industry peers and is often the most accurate and applicable information. You may also find good benchmark data from suppliers, customers, or direct competitors. We also suggest using web-based resources like Sageworks, which gather and share financial benchmarks for privately held business.

Your Financials

The financials may be the most reliable and unemotional source of data and information to help get to the realities of your business. As Jack Stack says, "The financials will speak to you, if you're willing to listen." We suggest you take a look at your three-to-five-year historical trends within five areas of financial performance—profit, cash, return, capitalization, and growth. Everyone wants a business model that can deliver a healthy profit, consistent cash, fair return, sufficient capital, and steady growth. As you review your financial trends, ask yourself these questions:

- How well are we driving profit?

- Are we generating enough cash?

- How well are we utilizing our assets?

- Are we getting a fair rate of return?

- Are we sufficiently capitalized?

- Considering all the above, can we steadily grow and expand the business?

The financials will help you answer these questions and many more. First, look at your year-over-year historical trends. Second, look at your performance compared to your industry or competitive benchmarks. And finally, discuss the strengths and weaknesses that emerge. What are the stories behind the numbers?

We suggest you download our practice assessment, input survey, and financial analysis tools and give them a try. You can find them at www.greatgame.com/gigtools.

Organize and Discuss the Issues

Get the Design Team together, and review the information you have gathered from the input surveys, financial analysis, and marketplace benchmarks. Organize the issues identified by our four views—Financial, Marketplace, Operations, and People—by writing each of the four views on a piece of flip-chart paper and capturing the issues for each area.

Step through each view. For example, begin by walking through the People and Operations view first. Use the specific results from the input survey. Be sure that both the employees' and managements' input are included and discussed. In fact, look closely at the different perspectives of both the leaders and the employees. Look for patterns, agreement, and gaps between what management believes is critical and what the employees see as critical. There is a lot to learn from the comparison of each perspective.

Remember—perception is reality … until it's not. Have a healthy, candid discussion around the issues identified. Try not to get defensive. Listen to your people, and let them tell you what they see as the critical issues of the company. We need to use this time to get aligned, and we can only do that if we take the time to educate *each other* on the true realities of the business. Here are some questions to consider:

- What input is aligned (meaning both management and employees agree)?

- What is not aligned?

- What is the reality?

- What are some issues that management identified but employees didn't?

- What are some issues that employees identified but management failed to mention?

- How big is the gap in perception?

Next, walk your team through the Financial and Marketplace views. Capture the strengths and weaknesses in the company's financial trends and opportunities for improvement based on the marketplace benchmark data. Remember, the real magic isn't in the Critical Number; it's in the *process* of getting to the Critical Number. This process alone will help build buy-in and commitment. It can also be a great source of financial education for your team.

You should now have the top issues from each business area

collected from actual company data and direct input from both management and employees.

Prioritize the Top Issues

Hand out sticky notes to each member of your team, and ask everyone to write down their top five issues from the discussion—five issues in total—considering all business views. Write only one issue per sticky note.

A quick way to organize and prioritize all the items is to ask the first person finished to place their five issues (five sticky notes) in a horizontal line on the wall. As others finish, they add their sticky notes underneath like items and create new columns for new issues.

Before moving on, make sure to ask yourself, "What is missing?" It's not unusual for this level of discussion to open up more issues. Give a final call for any new issues that might have emerged. Each should be written on a sticky note and placed on the wall.

Once everyone's issues are shared and compiled, a visual representation of initial agreement (the more sticky notes for the same issue, the more aligned the group is around that issue) and a sense of prioritization emerges. Now, determine the top five critical issues, and place each issue on the line-of-sight tool in its respective area—Financial, Marketplace, Operations, or People. This should give the team a clear view of the top issues facing the company and their potential impact on the overall financial results of the business.

The process now turns from issue *prioritization* to issue *assessment*—and ultimately the selection of a critical issue that not only resonates with the team but also is consistent with the realities of the business.

Brainstorm some potential Critical Numbers. Begin by asking your team this simple question: "What is one thing we can achieve in the next six to twelve months that would have the greatest single impact on the overall performance of the business?"

IT IS WHAT IT IS

The Critical Number is the Critical Number. Don't fall into the trap of attempting to pick a number that everyone directly influences in the hopes of involvement and more engagement. We actually see this a lot. For example, many companies quickly jump to profit in an effort to connect everyone to the Critical Number. They argue that it's the fastest way to get everyone in The Game, because everyone can impact profit in some way. This is all true, and they make a good point. In fact, most of the first-year Great Game practitioners will often just stick with profit as their first Critical Number. We are not debating that this may be a good place to start.

However, as you grow as a Great Game practitioner, you want your people focused on what will strengthen the company first. If that's profit, great. If it is something else that becomes critical, then don't hesitate to give that challenge to your people and let them fix it. In fact, many long-term Great Game practitioners choose profit as one of two Critical Numbers. The second Critical Number is the weakness they are trying to eliminate. This was demonstrated well in the evolution of Critical Numbers in ReGen Technologies. The ultimate objective is to identify what is absolutely critical to success—what clearly defines winning for the company at any given time.

Selecting the Critical Number

Use the following questions to help your Design Team make the final selection of your Critical Number:

1. Is the Critical Number feasible?

   a. Does the company have (or can they get) the resources, skills, time, and support needed to achieve the Critical Number?

2. Is the Critical Number impactful?

   a. Financial impact: Will the Critical Number keep people focused on the fundamentals of business—making money and generating cash?

   b. Strategic impact: Will the Critical Number make the company stronger and healthier by eliminating weaknesses and growing strategically?

   c. Educational impact: Will the Critical Number help educate people about the different aspects of the business and teach people exactly what it takes to be successful?

3. Is the Critical Number timely?

   a. Does the Critical Number represent something that needs to be done now, or are there other things that need to be done first?

   b. Does it need to be done quickly, before things get worse or the window closes?

Once you have selected your Critical Number, the next step in the process is to communicate and educate your people on the Critical Number. Use the following questions to develop your communication and education plan. This will help you align your team members to the importance of the Critical Number and how their input provided direction in the selection of the Critical Number. These questions will also help you start the education around the Critical Number.

- Critical to success
  - Why is the Critical Number important to the company's success?
  - Your people's success?
- Reality based
  - What issues discussed in the business review process supports the selection of the Critical Number?
- Impactful
  - How will this Critical Number make an impact on the company?
- Team supported
  - How has the team been included in the selection of the Critical Number?
- Increasingly important
  - If you do nothing with the Critical Number, what would be the impact to the company?
- Common goal
  - Who can directly or indirectly impact the Critical Number?
- Attainable
  - Is the achievement of the Critical Number reasonable and achievable?
- Learning opportunity
  - What increased business literacy can be realized by focusing on the Critical Number?

BRINGING IT ALL TOGETHER

When facilitating a "Path to Critical Number" session, remember to emphasize the selection of a Critical Number that keeps people focused on the fundamentals of business: making money and generating cash. A good Critical Number makes a company stronger by eliminating a weakness and supporting strategic growth. The best Critical Numbers also educate people about the different aspects of the business and teach them exactly what it takes to win! The Game is all about opportunities. The Critical Number provides an opportunity to learn and to win (two of our favorite things!) that becomes part of our everyday process of running a business.

Having gone through the process with your Design Team, you can now see that all this work, the process itself, is as powerful as the number itself. In the process, you don't just get a Critical Number but also the buy-in and understanding that is absolutely critical to execution—and success.

Download the Practice Assessment, Input Survey, Financial Analysis Tool, Line of Sight Tool, and Critical Number Communication Tool at www.greatgame.com/gigtools.

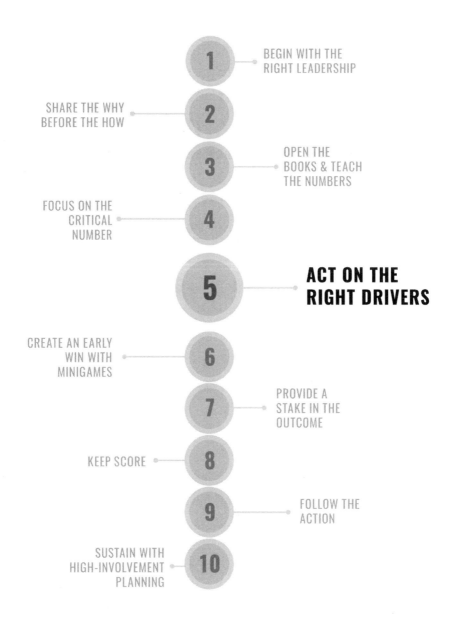

1 — BEGIN WITH THE RIGHT LEADERSHIP

2 — SHARE THE WHY BEFORE THE HOW

3 — OPEN THE BOOKS & TEACH THE NUMBERS

4 — FOCUS ON THE CRITICAL NUMBER

5 — ACT ON THE RIGHT DRIVERS

6 — CREATE AN EARLY WIN WITH MINIGAMES

7 — PROVIDE A STAKE IN THE OUTCOME

8 — KEEP SCORE

9 — FOLLOW THE ACTION

10 — SUSTAIN WITH HIGH-INVOLVEMENT PLANNING

STEP 5

ACT ON THE RIGHT DRIVERS

**Create line of sight, and ask people what they
can do today to make a difference.**

Once your people know what's critical to success, they must
then understand what they can do to *drive* that success.
Identifying the Right Drivers helps everyone begin to
understand what they can do—both individually and as a
team—to influence the Critical Number. It gives them *line of sight*
from their daily actions and decisions directly to the most important
goals of the organization.

Since at first many (or most) employees may not be familiar with
reading and acting on financial information, nonfinancial drivers or
measures are the key to teaching managers and employees how to
connect their work to the financial outcomes of the company.

Consider ReGen's Critical Number of return on assets described
in the previous chapter. Return on assets, or ROA, is a financial ratio
that tells us how well a company is using its assets (e.g., equipment,
inventory, etc.) and is a direct reflection of the company's ability to
generate cash. But what happened next? How did they take it to
the shop floor?

Getting people in every corner of the company to think about how they could move the needle on ROA is a matter of identifying the Right Drivers—in other words, the specific strategies that could be acted on to directly affect ROA. Every department across the company—from sales to materials—identified its respective drivers, including enhanced inventory management, better buying, controlled capital spending, and improved shop efficiencies. When you get everyone working together, focused on the Critical Number, and acting on the Right Drivers, ROA doesn't stand a chance of *not* improving.

THE CRITICAL NUMBER
Return on Assets

Role	Role	Role	Role
Sales	Production	Engineering	Materials
The Right Drivers	**The Right Drivers**	**The Right Drivers**	**The Right Drivers**
Focus on high GM customers /products	Produce only what we need	Control capital spending	Make better buys
Sell what we have in stock	Beat the labor standard	Reduce design flaws & scrap	Reduce inventory levels
Measures	**Measures**	**Measures**	**Measures**
25% min. customer gross margin	labor performance variance	< 24 month ROI	Purchase price variance
96% Fill Rate		< 1% Scrap Rate	>6x Inventory Turns

Figure 9

83

LINE OF SIGHT

Line of sight is simply a clear, unobstructed view to a target. Whether you are a surveyor, sharpshooter, or businessperson, how can you hit a target you can't see?

Ultimately, choosing the Right Drivers is all about creating line of sight. After all, isn't one of the primary objectives of GGOB to engage as many people as possible in learning and driving the business?

And how do you pick the Right Drivers to get optimal buy-in, commitment, and execution? Rather than cascade goals, targets, and metrics to your people, why not give them the education to align *themselves* to the most important goals of the business (the Critical Numbers)?

Repeat our mantra: *people support what they help create.* Why not *ask*? People who set their own goals tend to hit them.

ACT ON THE RIGHT DRIVERS: KERBEY LANE CAFÉ

Kerbey Lane Café in Austin, Texas, is renowned for making awesome pancakes and killer queso. Opening the books made a big impact on a young associate team leader named Matt, a millennial with plenty of ink on his arms and metal in his ears. He discovered that the restaurant he worked at lost some 150 spoons every week. He knew, because he counted them. Every. Single. Spoon.

He took ownership of line items like bread, dairy, and smallwares. He discovered that there was no "par" or standard for things like plates and silverware. So, he set standards, kept inventory, and learned. What really stuck out to him were spoons. He learned that the spoons they were losing cost only five dollars a dozen, so it wouldn't seem like a big deal to the average employee. But not to Matt. He understood that every dollar spent made an impact. He calculated that six hundred spoons a month is fifty dozen a year, or about $3,000. But they had seven restaurants in Austin. That was an unnecessary cost of $21,000 a year!

So, he figured out a process he could teach the six other restaurants to save this waste. There was even a theme of "No Spoon Left Behind." He understood, as did the other stores, that seemingly small things had an impact far beyond the savings. At a profitability of ten cents, the Kerbey Lane Café team would have to sell $210,000 in pancakes in order to offset just the lost spoons! Other teams focused on things like bacon, sodas, and paper products, resulting in a revenue "offset" impact of over $1 million in the first year.

• • •

How's that for the power of creating a line of sight between what people do every day and the bottom line?

So, how many "spoons" do you have in your organization?

The point of this chapter is to begin to show each and every employee how and where they fit in the big financial picture of the business and, most importantly, how they can immediately make an impact on the Critical Number. That's creating line of sight.

Now it's time to create an early win. Your people now have a clear line of sight to what they can do to make a difference. Let's equip them and empower them to use that newfound knowledge to improve the business. Everybody should focus on the goal of The Game: the Critical Number. But the only way we can achieve the goal of The Game is by acting on the everyday activities and behaviors (like the drivers you identified above) that influence the Critical Number. How do you start making things happen immediately? By giving people a chance to win early and win often. With MiniGames, we believe that small wins add up to big wins.

Download the Driver Worksheet at www.greatgame.com/gigtools.

1   BEGIN WITH THE RIGHT LEADERSHIP

2   SHARE THE WHY BEFORE THE HOW

3   OPEN THE BOOKS & TEACH THE NUMBERS

4   FOCUS ON THE CRITICAL NUMBER

5   ACT ON THE RIGHT DRIVERS

CREATE AN EARLY WIN WITH MINIGAMES   6

7   PROVIDE A STAKE IN THE OUTCOME

8   KEEP SCORE

9   FOLLOW THE ACTION

10   SUSTAIN WITH HIGH-INVOLVEMENT PLANNING

CREATE AN EARLY WIN WITH MINIGAMES

Give people a chance to win early and often.

Having identified your Critical Number and the Right Drivers that influence it, you now can give your team a chance to create an early win with MiniGames. With targeted day-to-day improvements that add up to long-term success, MiniGames bring a laser focus to those small, everyday wins that put us that much closer to the big win.

Not a day goes by that we don't hear someone in The Great Game community telling us a story about how their frontline people have astounded them with creativity, innovation, and dogged determination to achieve a goal. Most of this praise surrounds one of our favorite practices: MiniGames.

Once you've seen the transformational power of The Great Game of Business, your team will begin to grab on to the gamification aspects and, along with them, the language. Words like Huddles, Scoreboards, and so on will become part of the vernacular of your organization.

MiniGames are a powerful example of gamification.

CREATE AN EARLY WIN WITH MINIGAMES: ROLF GLASS

Rolf Glass is a manufacturer of decorative glass located in Mount Pleasant, Pennsylvania. Its skilled team of operators employs a variety of processes to create its designs, such as sandblast etching, diamond wheel engraving, and glass polishing.

When the operators at Rolf reviewed their work at their company-wide, all-hands Huddle, they learned that their machines were operating at just 88 percent efficiency—which meant they were losing 12 percent of their potential profits due to a lack of productivity. If they could boost their efficiency, they could drive their Critical Number of profitability and add up to $144,000 in profits to their bottom line for the year.

In other words, the team identified that increasing machine operator efficiency was an important driver to improved productivity and their Critical Number of profitability. As the team members discussed that missed opportunity, they focused on their key constraint: when the machine operators didn't load or unload their machine efficiently, productivity suffered.

In many companies, the solution would be to simply tell the operators they were underperforming and order them to become more efficient. While that might create a short-term gain, it rarely results in lasting change.

But at Rolf, they knew of a better and far more effective way to improve. They created a MiniGame. The beauty of MiniGames is that they require teamwork to win and help bridge the gap between management and employees. Along the way, MiniGames provide incentives for employees to change processes, systems, and behaviors to get results—while having fun at the same time.

Management got the operators involved in creating the

MiniGame. The team discussed what a reasonable improvement goal would be and agreed upon a target of operating at 95 percent efficiency for a period of nine weeks. They chose a fun golfing theme for their MiniGame that would be reflected in their scoreboard as well as their rewards.

They created a scoreboard that looked like a nine-hole golf course (figure 10), with a golf ball as their game piece. It was simple and fun to look at, making it easy to see at a glance how the team was progressing. Each week the team played The Game, the golf ball would move to the next hole on the course. After four weeks, the team would end up at the clubhouse—where they could earn partial rewards and recognition for progress they made up to that point.

If the team had reached its partial goal at the end of the fourth week, the company would host a cookout at the end of the month. If the team maintained its efficiency goal after nine weeks, they would enjoy a picnic held at a local amusement park.

This MiniGame included goals for both the team and for individuals. Operators who ran their machines at 100 percent efficiency three times in a single week—something they called a "benchmark birdie"—would earn a gift card to use at the amusement park.

Also, for every week the team achieved its goal of operating at 95 percent efficiency—something they called a "hole in one"—operators would become eligible for prizes that would be drawn at the picnic held at the end of the month.

EFFICIENCY PAR FORE THE COURSE

Figure 10

The "course" on the scoreboard also contained sand traps and water hazards. Anytime the team's efficiency slipped—or quality or rework issues cropped up—the game piece would slide into a hazard. That would then trigger additional team Huddles and coaching from supervisors to help get the team back on course.

Every Monday, the team gathered in a series of Huddles to update the status of their progress as well as to discuss strategies and best practices to win The Game. When they began, the team was worried that the individual-operator weekly "birdie" goals of 100 percent might be too difficult. But not only did they prove to be achievable, they also provided benchmarks and inspiration for the other operators as they shared these best practices across the entire team. Overall, the team exceeded its efficiency goal for the first month—which meant they got to celebrate that accomplishment with a cookout. By the end of the ninth week, they nailed their goal—achieving an efficiency of 98.5 percent—and earned their celebratory picnic and the chance to earn one of nine raffle prizes given out at the amusement park.

While management was concerned that the efficiency gains would only be temporary—that operators would just go back to their old routines after the MiniGame ended—the opposite happened. Efficiency remained steady at more than 98 percent over the next few months (see figure 11). Not to mention, the operators now knew that they were capable of operating at a level they had thought unachievable before.

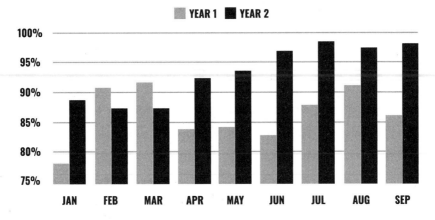

Figure 11

The efficiency increase not only generated an additional $25,800 in profits for the business in just nine weeks, it also helped improve the company's culture. None of this could have been accomplished without the improved teamwork from all involved or the commitment to help one another and find ways to do things differently and better. That's the real, lasting payoff from playing MiniGames.

• • •

WHY PLAY MINIGAMES?

Playing MiniGames is a relatively simple practice that can create powerful engagement and bottom-line results. MiniGames are like small incentive plans targeted at day-to-day improvements that add up to year-end success. They're played to effect a change, reinforce business education, build teamwork, and create a culture of winning—all of which lead to success for the company and for the players.

Effect a Change

The primary reason for playing a MiniGame is to strengthen the business by driving results through improved performance. MiniGames help companies boost work-group, departmental, and corporate performance by focusing on an operational or financial number that represents a weakness or an opportunity. MiniGame teams are challenged to find solutions to current problems and take advantage of current opportunities—whatever it takes to get to the goal! The best MiniGames effect a change in a system, process, or behavior that will stick long after the MiniGame is over.

Reinforce Business Education

MiniGames are one of the most effective tools used to build a business of businesspeople. MiniGames provide the opportunity for employees to practically apply the business education they receive and to learn even more as they play. Since many (or most) employees are unfamiliar with reading and acting on financial information, MiniGames focused on nonfinancial drivers or measures are the key to teaching managers and employees how to connect their work to the financial outcomes of the company. MiniGames also reinforce key principles and practices of The Game. Employees learn to set goals, keep score, run effective Huddles, practice forward forecasting, and hold each other accountable, experiencing The Big Game in microcosm.

Build Teamwork

MiniGames provide the people on a team (work group or department) with a shared common goal. While individual contribution is valued, individuals must unite as a team in order to reach the goal. MiniGame rewards are based on the success of the team. The shared reward gives each player a vested interest in helping the team achieve its goal. MiniGames underscore the concept that we're all in this together. It's the number we are competing against, not each other. Through MiniGames, employees learn that a united team is vital to success at every level of the company.

As a short-term version of The Great Game, MiniGames also reinforce key components of team success—goal setting, mutual responsibility, and performance management—by teaching players to track, measure, and report team activity by showing them how they can contribute to team success and by rewarding them when they do.

Create a Culture of Winning

Face it—most people don't wake up feeling like winners. Life's hard. Maybe, just maybe, we could create a winning environment at work in which people are recognized and results are rewarded. MiniGames instill the desire to win and, if used often, can help create a culture of winning. The more MiniGames are played, the more opportunities employees have to win. The more employees win, the more they *want* to win. Why not make winning a habit?

MINIGAME DESIGN STEPS

Thoughtful design and proper preparation will help you avoid common pitfalls and create a winning MiniGame with your team. There are ten proven steps to designing a successful and effective MiniGame:

1. Select the objective.

2. Set the improvement goal.

3. Estimate the benefit.

4. Identify the players.

5. Determine the time frame.

6. Create a theme.

7. Build a scoreboard, and establish a Huddle rhythm.

8. Decide on the rewards, and determine an award schedule.

9. Play The Game.

10. Celebrate the win.

Coach's tip: As you get started, consider implementing more than one MiniGame, each in a different work group. You'll have more opportunities for early success and deeper learning.

Step 1: Select the Objective

What do we want to achieve? Put it into words. While drivers that directly influence the Critical Number are often your best choice for effective MiniGames, other problems or opportunities for improvement can also be rewarding. Are there organic issues and challenges that are frustrating your team every day? In the Rolf Glass story, the team discovered that operator efficiency was a key driver to their Critical Number of profitability. Their objective became improving productivity through operator efficiency.

Step 2: Set the Improvement Goal

How will we measure success? Put a number on it. Once the objective has been selected, an improvement goal must be set. An objective without measurement is just fantasy, and The Game is founded firmly in reality.

Make sure the goal is achievable. People won't play a game if they don't think they can win. First, determine your "as is" state of performance. The team's past performance and industry benchmarks can also serve as baselines. Whatever the baseline is, get the team involved in setting the improvement goal. Ask the team, "What's possible? What do you think we can actually pull off?" They're the ones who must believe that it's reasonable and achievable if you want to see them really get engaged.

You'll remember that Rolf Glass knew its past performance of 88 percent left money on the table that could be going to the company (and the bonus pool!).

Management and the operators decided as a team that they would shoot for 95 percent efficiency with a stretch goal of 100 percent. So, "from 88 percent efficiency to 95 percent efficiency in nine weeks" became their improvement goal.

"X to Y by when" is Goal Setting 101. In other words, tell me where you are, where you're going, and when you plan to get there.

Here's another important point. In the following examples, which is better? "We're going to reduce waste by fifty percent" or "We're going to reduce waste from four thousand dollars a month to two thousand dollars a month, and we'll do it in ninety days."

You guessed it. The latter puts waste into terms everyone can understand. People get paid in dollars, not percentages. Mind you, we still want to teach people percentages—so why not do both? It's important to note that this example—waste—brings to mind a manufacturing issue. But waste affects all businesses; just change the word *waste* to *inefficiency* or *rework*, or choose another term. There is one universal truth in business: we all have the same problems.

> *Coach's tip: If current performance is not being accurately and reliably measured, you could design a "learning" MiniGame to get a baseline in the first thirty days, improve it, and maintain that performance for the next sixty to ninety days.*

Step 3: Estimate the Benefit

If you really want to build a business of businesspeople, teach them business at every turn. Once they establish the objective and the "X to Y by when" improvement goal, ask them to estimate the benefit to the business, both in financial and cultural results. Involving the team in estimating the benefit is a great way of sorting out the MiniGames we should do today and those not worth playing. It's a vetting process and a business education opportunity. What's the biggest bang for the buck? We can explore ideas together about how to make the biggest impact as opposed to a manager just saying no.

For Rolf Glass, the team calculated there was $28,500 in additional profits if they maintained 95 percent operator efficiency in nine weeks—a potential annual improvement of over $150,000!

Rolf management also had an early concern that when the MiniGame was completed, the efficiency would backslide without continued focus. What they underestimated were the changes in behaviors and the new ways their operators developed to improve their efficiency. So, in the months following the completion of the MiniGame, their efficiency ran 98.2 percent and 98.4 percent respectively, well above their original goal (refer to figure 11).

If you set up a game that creates a change in a habit, behavior, or process, you not only achieve rapid results but also create a lasting change. We call this the MiniGame Effect. (More on this at the end of this chapter.) There's a step change between what the performance was at the start of The Game and what it is after The Game. That performance will continue on because you may have changed the activities, processes, and behaviors that were causing that lower performance.

Step 4: Identify the Players

Here's an easy one: Who can move the number? Who can impact the objective? A MiniGame is most often played by a natural team—a work group, department, functional group, or geographic unit. If an individual has the ability to directly impact the MiniGame goal—if they have line of sight—they're on the team.

At some point, you'll likely want to have multiple MiniGames going on at once. The rule of thumb is focus. It's fine to have multiple MiniGames, but try not to have one person in more than one MiniGame at a time.

For Rolf, it was clear that the machine operators were the natural team, supported by supervisors and management.

Step 5: Determine the Time Frame

Which of the gurus are right? You've heard "twenty-one days to a new habit" or "the sixty-six-day challenge." Some behavioral scientists tell us that it takes six weeks to change behavior.

What's the right duration to really make your MiniGame work

best?

Keep it simple. Just make sure it's long enough to change a behavior and short enough to keep people interested. You want your team to win early and win often. In nearly forty years of practice in thousands of companies, we have found six weeks to ninety days to be the range (ninety days being most popular). Sure, yours could be one month or four. Just ask the question, "What does this Game require?"

> *Coach's tip: If hitting the goal may take longer than ninety days to achieve, consider creating two back-to-back games— for example, level 1 and level 2 MiniGames—to keep people interested and engaged. Change up the theme, scoreboard, or rewards. Rolf Glass had the opportunity to take its "nine holes in nine weeks" golf theme to a level 2 MiniGame, playing the "back nine" with enhanced rewards.*

Step 6: Create a Theme

In the first steps, we're defining the objective and establishing the goal. Now, we're bringing it to life! One of the most engaging elements of MiniGames is the theme. Sometimes the goal itself will inspire a theme. It could be the strategy the team is using to get there or perhaps the prize its members are pulling for. Maybe even the time of year. One of the best sources of inspiration can be pop culture—memes, music, or movies. What's happening in the world?

Whatever the theme, ask these questions:

- Is it inspiring, engaging, and fun?

- Whose theme is it? (Remember, *people support what they help create!*)

- Is it memorable?

- Does the theme carry through the scoreboard and rewards?

Rolf's team chose a golf theme, which tied beautifully into the group's interests, the scoreboard, and the rewards (minigolf at the amusement park).

Step 7: Build a Scoreboard, and Establish a Huddle Rhythm

An engaging theme usually inspires the greatest scoreboards, and an effective scoreboard is one that is simple and easy to understand. While MiniGame scoreboards must track the numbers associated with The Game, avoid scoreboards that are so detailed they overwhelm players with too much information. Sure, have a spreadsheet to track, measure, and report, but MiniGame scoreboards should communicate if you are winning or losing in three seconds or less.

Consider Rolf's simple golf course scoreboard with its traveling golf ball game piece. Holes in one and birdies represented performance beyond the 95 percent standard the team had set. Sand traps and water hazards represented drops in efficiency, flagging the need for help. Winning or losing was immediately evident and highly visible to everyone.

The best MiniGame scoreboards are frequently viewed and updated by the team playing the MiniGame. In order to keep players focused on the results of their performance, a MiniGame scoreboard should be updated daily, or perhaps even by shift, if applicable. Posting the scoreboard in an area where it can be easily viewed keeps the players motivated and informed about what it takes to win.

Coach's tip: You don't care what the scoreboard looks like or whether it has pipe cleaners, glitter, or construction paper. You care if your team members are learning something—if they feel like they can make a difference. Remember the ugly baby syndrome: "Nobody loves an ugly baby like its mama." If your people build it, they'll care for it.

EFFICIENCY PAR FORE THE COURSE

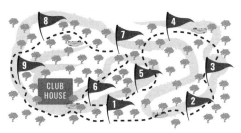

People support what they help create.

As your MiniGame progresses, regular communication through the scoreboard and Huddles is vital to success. Team members need to see a direct tie between their actions and the score of the MiniGame (*that's* line of sight). Seeing the numbers on the scoreboard change as a result of their performance establishes that tie.

Rolf's weekly Huddles gave individuals a constant connection to how the entire production team was performing. Ad hoc Huddles were held when folks found themselves in a sand trap or water hazard. Halfway through the MiniGame, they took time to recognize the players and celebrate their progress with a cookout.

Your Huddle timing will depend on your MiniGame. For longer time frames, weekly Huddles are appropriate. For shorter games, brief daily stand-up Huddles will keep the energy focused.

Create an atmosphere in your MiniGame Huddles where learning is emphasized and questions are encouraged but where gripes and complaints are not. Huddling around a MiniGame scoreboard gives the team an opportunity to review the status of the MiniGame, to brainstorm ideas for continued improvement, and to get fired up.

Step 8: Decide on the Rewards, and Determine an Award Schedule

Rolf Glass scored significant improvements in efficiency and captured tens of thousands of dollars in savings. The rewards were cookouts and amusement parks. Why didn't anyone demand a piece of the pie? A cut of the profits? Ask anybody what they want as a reward, and what do you think they'll say?

"Gimme cash." Every time, guaranteed.

But think twice about cash. While cash is understood by everyone and easy to administer, it is not a memorable reward. It has no trophy value. Cash is often used to pay bills and is then quickly forgotten. Cash also tends to become an "expected" reward and therefore does little to motivate any change in behavior—and quickly becomes an entitlement. With MiniGame rewards, ***don't set this precedent***. When you fully implement The Great Game, employees will understand that any financial gains created from MiniGame wins will fund their annual bonus plan—a bonus plan that will be worth significantly more than short-term MiniGame rewards.

The folks at Rolf did a great job reinforcing the team's Stake in the Outcome by awarding modest prizes and recognition for the wins of their MiniGame. Larger rewards were earned from a bonus plan based on overall company success. But there's more.

They also aligned the efforts of their team to a larger purpose for the organization, providing a sustainable place to work with job security and career opportunities.

The first step in choosing rewards for a MiniGame is pretty simple: ***Ask them what they want***. *People support what they help create.* Based on the effort it will take to achieve the goal and the estimated benefit, what would be reasonable? In our experience, people will generally ask for far less than you think they will. And if they don't, it's a great coaching opportunity. If you're teaching people business, and they understand how hard it is to make money, it's an adult conversation.

So, if it's not cash, what do we do? Focus the team on fun, memorable, motivating rewards. To truly motivate, you must provide a reward that the players genuinely value to inspire performance. Sometimes bragging rights alone will suffice. It's amazing what people will compete for! A memorable prize is one that anchors the memory of the accomplishment. We like to call this "trophy value"—something tangible, a reminder of the achievement that can be remembered long after the celebration.

Alternatives to cash could include the following:

- Meals

- Time off

- Movie tickets

- Gift cards

- Lottery tickets

- Trophies

- Maid services

- Company logo prizes

- Group activities

- A turn at a prize wheel

- Travel vouchers

- Spa services

- Tickets to a sporting event

Coach's tip: These days, gift cards are popular, but these are still a cash equivalent. If you do find yourself giving gift cards, require each team member to share with the group what they bought!

Next you'll want to set an award schedule. Here's what a ninety-day MiniGame reward system might look like: If your people themed their MiniGame around their favorite sports team, the thirty-day reward could be a team ball cap. The sixty-day reward could be a jersey emblazoned with their beloved theme. And the ninety-day reward could be a group celebration at the local AAA park on the club level. Something they may never do on their own and will never forget.

A simple way to think about progressive rewards is by breaking them down into small, medium, and large.

SET AN AWARD SCHEDULE

30	60	90
S	M	L
REASONABLE	ACHIEVABLE	STRETCH
HOT DOG	HAMBURGER	STEAK

Figure 12

You may tie them in to performance levels such as reasonable, achievable, or stretch. If it's food, think of them as hot dog, hamburger, or steak levels. These progressive reward levels allow you to engineer early wins and create momentum. It also allows you to reward incremental improvements so you can avoid "all or nothing" goals.

These simple guidelines will help you and your team plan out your entire MiniGame reward system.

Your MiniGame may not fall conveniently into a thirty-, sixty-, or ninety-day schedule. It may be tied to the progress toward the goal rather than the calendar. The first reward at Rolf was an entry into a prize drawing, and the second reward was a cookout scheduled at four weeks. The group celebration at the amusement park was at the nine-week mark. Whatever your schedule, involve your team in the planning of the goal, scoreboard, theme, and rewards.

How much do you share with the team? Relax. This is way better for you than you think. For easy math, let's say your MiniGame is forecast to provide everyone on the team one hundred dollars in rewards. How would you split that up between a small, a medium, and a large prize? One permutation would be as follows: small—ten dollars; medium—twenty dollars; and large—seventy dollars.

Now you have a budget for the first thirty days of your MiniGame, the second thirty days, and the final thirty days, culminating in the largest reward.

Step 9: Play The Game

It's important to roll out a MiniGame with enthusiasm. Someone must take ownership of keeping the spirit alive, preferably a member of the team playing the MiniGame. Again, people support what they help create. Keep the scoreboard updated, keep up the Huddles, and celebrate every small win along the way. Play The Game with enthusiasm. A well-promoted MiniGame is a successful one.

Step 10: Celebrate the Win

You would be surprised to learn how often people forget to celebrate the win and recognize the players. Well-designed MiniGames have celebrations built into the reward system. It may be one that generates good feelings that can be remembered weeks, months, or even years after the goal was achieved and the reward received. The opportunity to celebrate with teammates is an example of the feel-good factor. Give the team a chance to revel in its accomplishment. When handled correctly, the good feelings created can far surpass the monetary value of the prize.

Just don't get "too busy" to stop and reflect on what the team has accomplished and to pay out the rewards. You'll find it's the best way to memorialize the win.

At Rolf Glass, the rewards and recognition were tied to a company picnic celebration at a local amusement park. At Rolf's outing, they raffled off nine prizes, each commemorating weekly successes they experienced during the MiniGame. They literally tied rewards directly to the behaviors that earned the rewards.

THE MINIGAME EFFECT: PRACTICE VELOCITY

You want your team to design MiniGames that create rapid results and lasting change. Consider the example of a company called Practice Velocity, which was founded "by doctors, for doctors" in 2002. Practice Velocity provides software, teleradiology, and revenue-cycle management services to more than 2,400 urgent-care clinics across all fifty states.

Prior to playing GGOB, staff members had no access to budgets or any insight into their ability to influence numbers. Employees made financial decisions by running them up the ladder to leadership. Now, thanks to The Game, team members feel empowered to make decisions. Best of all, they feel proud when they find ways to save money while still providing exceptional customer service and delivering a ten-point increase in client net promoter score.

From the start, MiniGames were a hit, driving employee engagement and real-life lessons on how each team player affected company outcomes. Successful MiniGames focused on areas such as increasing sales leads, growing the number of referrals for hiring new employees, and even raising the percentage of employees getting flu shots. "The Great Game taught us that MiniGames are about creating new habits," says CEO Dr. David Stern. "Habits are not about results. Habits are what you do every day."

The key to the success of those MiniGames was that they were built around behaviors and activities, defined as the key measurable actions that drive the Critical Number. For instance, rather than focusing a MiniGame on increasing sales, members of the Practice Velocity sales team focused on something they do daily: software demos. Every week, the sales team looked at the demo numbers to gauge team success. "Paradoxically, focusing on lead measures, not just the end goal, has definitely made a big difference in achieving the end goal," says Stern. "Today, every Practice Velocity team makes better, more educated decisions based on data. They are learning and thinking about how each decision affects the company's bottom line and how it affects the client."

• • •

To put that another way, lasting, sustainable change occurs when you can change the behavior. That's the MiniGame effect.

THE MINIGAME EFFECT

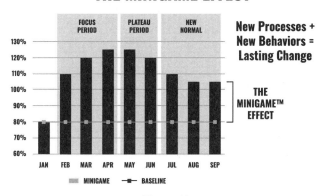

Figure 13

MINIGAME CHECKLIST

A well-designed MiniGame will satisfy this checklist:

- The MiniGame objective is meaningful to the company's overall performance.

- The "Win"—the improvement goal—is clearly defined and communicated.

- The players have "line of sight" to the targeted goal and know the financial benefit to the company of improving their performance.

- The team is competing against a problem or opportunity, not each other.

- The time-frame is limited in duration, or incremental goals/prizes are utilized.

- Long-term change in behaviors, processes, or systems is promoted.

- The scoreboard can be easily and frequently scored and is simple and easy to understand.

- Huddles are scheduled to review the scoreboard and keep the team (including offsite employees) focused on and informed about the MiniGame.

- Prizes are memorable and meaningful.

- Prizes reward performance, not motivate participation.

- The MiniGame has a theme—title, scoreboard, prizes—that supports promotion and the creation of a memory of winning.

- Business training is incorporated to aid understanding.

- Negative outcomes for other workgroups/departments have been considered.

- A scorekeeper has been appointed to settle disputes.

Download the MiniGame Design Tool and the MiniGame Checklist at www.greatgame.com/gigtools

1 BEGIN WITH THE RIGHT LEADERSHIP

2 SHARE THE WHY BEFORE THE HOW

3 OPEN THE BOOKS & TEACH THE NUMBERS

4 FOCUS ON THE CRITICAL NUMBER

5 ACT ON THE RIGHT DRIVERS

6 CREATE AN EARLY WIN WITH MINIGAMES

7 **PROVIDE A STAKE IN THE OUTCOME**

8 KEEP SCORE

9 FOLLOW THE ACTION

10 SUSTAIN WITH HIGH-INVOLVEMENT PLANNING

PROVIDE A STAKE IN THE OUTCOME

Define "What's in it for me," and communicate, communicate, communicate.

Johanna ohn Hughes must at some point in his life have been a part of a terrible bonus plan, or he never would have been able to write National Lampoon's *Christmas Vacation*. And people who never participated in a bad bonus plan can never fully appreciate Clark's plight.

Most bonus plans are disappointing to business owners because they don't motivate, they aren't appreciated, and they quickly become entitlements. Most bonus plans disappoint employees because they're a mystery, they're unpredictable, and they're never, ever enough.

Think about it. What was the premise of *Christmas Vacation*? Clark Griswold was digging a hole for a pool he could not afford, based on a bonus he wasn't sure he'd get. Whoa! Who would do that? Apparently everyone, if you look at US consumer debt.

The fact is, most bonus plans suck.

So many are discretionary or too complex. Some pit people against one another.

A few are impossible for employees to understand.

The worst one ever? The lotto bonus. When an owner has taken great pride in designing the ultimate bonus plan, but employees believe the odds are against them. And every day, they come to work, keep "scratching the tickets," but feel deep down that *there is no way they're ever gonna get it.*

Which one is yours?

Through the years, many pursued The Great Game of Business because they heard about the power of a bonus plan as a legendary "killer app"—something that would solve all their problems. But a bonus plan simply won't do that. Bonuses alone don't drive improved performance—people do. A bonus plan can help improve results only if people clearly understand what (and why) improvements are needed, how they can make a difference, and what they stand to gain.

From our experience, if any of these components are missing in your bonus plan, you might as well give out memberships to the "Jelly of the Month Club" and hope for the best.

In this chapter we'll cover the components of providing a Stake in the Outcome. It's one of the most evolved forms of capitalism. A Stake in the Outcome is an equitable system that connects the people who create the numbers and the results in the business with the rewards and recognition they deserve—while eliminating entitlement and resentment. When the team wins, the company wins.

Imagine a self-funding, progressive payout bonus program in which every employee could forecast their take each week after the all-team Huddle.

That is what a true Stake in the Outcome bonus plan is all about: a plan in which we protect the company's long-term sustainability first, put the rewards as close as possible to the behavior that earned the reward (to reinforce that winning behavior), and never pay a reward we have not yet earned.

While the concept of *good* bonus plans may seem simple, design and execution require some real work. Here are the most important design and implementation rules that embody The Great Game of Business philosophy on bonus plans.

The order in which you design a bonus plan is vital to its effectiveness. Think of these building blocks as if you were constructing a building. Let's begin with a strong foundation and work our way up.

BUILDING BLOCKS OF AN EFFECTIVE BONUS PLAN

CREATE EARLY WINS	COMMUNICATE	
Give people a chance to win early and often	COMMUNICATE COMMUNICATE	Always **celebrate** the win and **recognize** the players

	LINE-OF-SIGHT
RALLY PEOPLE AROUND A COMMON GOAL What is your Critical Number?	Use the bonus to teach people the business

GAIN-SHARE VS. PROFIT SHARE
Provide a significant portion of the gain

SELF-FUNDED
Ensure the company's financial security & improved value, FIRST

Figure 14

Building Blocks of a Good Bonus Plan

Here are the components of a good bonus plan:

- First, ensure long-term financial security of the company.

- Then, provide a significant portion of the gain.

- Rally people around a common goal: the Critical Number.

- Use the bonus plan to teach people about business.

- Give people a chance to win early and win often.

- Communicate, communicate, communicate.

- Always celebrate the win and recognize the players.

Ensure Long-Term Financial Security

Everyone must understand that the company's financial health is number one. Period. A healthy balance sheet means sustainability, and *that* ensures job security. Until the company is secure, no one should earn a bonus.

At SRC, for example, before we design our bonus plan, we first look at what investments we will need for the continued growth and sustainability of the business—working capital such as replacing worn-out equipment, investments in inventory, growth in receivables, debt reduction, and so on. All these investments must be covered first to ensure the company's health. We define this as our *threshold*—the minimum performance required to maintain the long-term financial security of the company.

What's *your* threshold? If a manufacturing company like SRC is earning 3 percent or less of sales, it's making a profit but may be *dying* as a company, because a 3 percent return doesn't generate the capital necessary to reinvest in the business. At 4 percent to 5 percent, it's generating just enough to make the investments to *survive*. At 6 percent and above, it's *thriving*, because it has sufficient profits to invest in the business and distribute a healthy return to the owners—and the employees who have earned a bonus.

What does your industry look like? What's your threshold?

When you develop your threshold, you will need to ask yourself, "What investments or outlays do we plan this year that are not already accounted for in our profit-and-loss statement?" Examples are capital expenditures, inventory, debt reduction, and so on. Here is a chart that illustrates this in dollars and will help you calculate your threshold (see figure 15).

The threshold should also include a fair return for the owner and other investors in the business. Remember, part of maintaining the financial security of the business is keeping the investors happy.

THRESHOLD CALCULATION EXAMPLE

Plan profit before tax=	**$250,000**
Taxes	($100,000)
Add back depreciation	$50,000
Change in accounts receivables	($25,000)
Change in inventory	$25,000
Capital expenditures	($75,000)
Debt payments (principle only)	($50,000)
Owners draw (i.e. dividends or additional retained earnings)	($25,000)
Savings (additional cash in the bank)	($25,000)
What's left?	$25,000
Required 'minimum' performance=	**$225,000**

Figure 15

In this example, the company has established a plan that generates $250,000 in profits for the year. In the chart, the expenditures you see below the profit line represent reinvestments that will secure the future of the company and its continued growth.

After all these reinvestments, the company shows $25,000 left over from the profits. So, the minimum amount of profits the company will need to generate to cover these investments and maintain the growth and security of the business is $225,000.

Any profit generated over this profit threshold can begin to fund a bonus pool.

Provide a Significant Portion of the Gain

Once you know what minimum profit is required to cover the threshold, any additional profits are available to fund other investments, including a bonus plan for your people. We prefer to think of this as a "gain share" program rather than a "profit share" program where companies share a percentage of every dollar of profit made. In other words, the bonus plan is completely self-funded by the "gain" over the threshold.

GAIN SHARING

| 50% TO COMPANY | 50% TO POOL | "GAIN" |

| 'THRESHOLD' |

Figure 16

117

We recommend that you allocate 50 percent of any additional profits above your threshold to a bonus pool. While this is not a hard and fast rule, the fifty/fifty split demonstrates true partnership between the organization and the team (see figure 16). Our intention is to provide as much as 10 percent to 20 percent of an employee's annual compensation, which represents one to two months of additional pay. This will get people's attention.

Some more generous owners ask, "Why can't we allocate every dollar over the threshold to a bonus payout? Haven't we covered all the needs of the business?"

Yes, you have covered all the *planned* needs of the business. But what about the potential *unplanned* needs? Also, if you are exceeding your threshold, it's a good guess that you're growing. And if you're growing, you'll need additional profits to invest in that growth.

Guess what? Over time, your people will begin to understand all this. They'll relate to the idea that profits generated in the business don't always end up in the owner's bank account and that many of the profits are reinvested to maintain growth and to secure good-paying jobs. They will appreciate that you have set aside bonuses that not only reflect the effort they've put in but also secured their future.

Rally People around a Common Goal

We want people to work together as a team—to pull in the same direction. We want to reinforce cooperation and encourage collective efforts to make the business stronger. We either win together, or we don't win at all.

Get everybody involved. To get real commitment and better results, people should be highly involved in the creation of their incentives. That's why the High-Involvement Planning process is so important. It's during this HIP process that we establish the rules of

The Game. We get everybody together to take stock of our situation, target specific improvements we need to make, and then commit to hitting those targets. The annual bonus plan is the result of these efforts.

An effective bonus plan should focus on improvement in one or two key performance targets: the Critical Numbers. The Critical Number, as you know, should represent a performance issue that at any given time is going to have the greatest impact on the business and is absolutely critical to success.

Many companies will almost always select profit as one of their Critical Numbers—to ensure people stay focused on making money. And profits are often the only reliable way to fund the bonus payouts. The other Critical Numbers will change from year to year, depending on what you see as your biggest vulnerability or strategic goal. We can then use the profits we generate (over threshold, of course) to reward the team for eliminating one of these vulnerabilities. In return, by eliminating the vulnerability, we strengthen the company and protect future profits.

Use the Bonus Plan to Teach People about Business

Your bonus plan can be the most effective education tool you have. Too often, employees don't understand the financial impact of their decisions and actions or, worse, their nondecisions and nonactions. So, by tying the bonus plan to the Critical Number and then educating people on how each and every one of them can contribute to achieving it, we teach and educate our people about the business. The objective is to help everybody create a line of sight from what they do every day to the overall financial results of the company.

We always hope for the upside in business—steady sales growth, increasing profits, and improved value. Yet this is not always the case.

In fact, too few employees understand the risks that always come along with the rewards. In many ways, The Game helps us encourage employees to check the entitlement attitude at the door and put the "What's in it for me?" in the right perspective, which is absolutely critical in any successful bonus plan.

Give People a Chance to Win Early and Win Often

Bonus plans should, above all, motivate people. And winning gets people motivated. The more people win, the more they want to win. So, it's important to structure your plan to create some early wins that get them in The Game—and keep them in The Game.

Put rewards close to the behaviors that earned the rewards. Annual bonuses are commonplace, with payouts coming out once a year and at the end of the year. This is never effective, because people forget what they did throughout the year to earn the reward. It defeats the purpose, providing no consistent link between performance and the reward. Start with small, frequent bonus payouts, and let them grow as performance continues to improve.

We use a time-tested "10–20–30–40" payout model. In the first quarter, we'll pay out 10 percent of what the team has earned in rewards year to date, regardless of what the bonus pool contains at that time. In the second quarter, 20 percent will be paid out of the available pool, and in the third quarter, 30 percent. And, of course, 40 percent in the fourth quarter (see figure 17).

PERIOD	PERIOD PAYOUT	YTD PAYOUT	% OF SALARY
1st Qtr.	10%	10%	1% to 20%
2nd Qtr.	20%	30%	1% to 20%
3rd Qtr.	30%	60%	1% to 20%
4th Qtr.	40%	100%	1% to 20%

Figure 17

This plan is not only progressive but also cumulative. In other words, if we have a crummy Q1 and Q2 but rally in Q3 (attaining our year-to-date goal), we could earn the 10 percent, 20 percent, *and* the 30 percent rewards, totaling 60 percent of the available pool.

The progressive nature of the "10–20–30–40" plan has helped businesses in every industry. Many seasonal businesses like it because it protects the company from a cash crunch but gets people in The Game early and keeps them engaged with frequent (and progressively bigger) quarterly payouts.

Coach's Tip: When talking about the bonus with your team, remember to communicate in currency everyone can easily relate to—hours, days, dollars. People don't get paid in percentages. While a 10 percent discount at the local store may not seem like much of a deal, 10 percent of earnings is 5.2 weeks! That's 26 days of pay ... or 208 hours (see figure 18)! Now that's something people can talk about after work.

1% to 3%	Early Win	2.6 to 7.8 days
5% to 8%	Reasonable	3 to 4 weeks
10% to 12%	Achievable	5.2 to 6.2 weeks
15% to 20%	Stretch	7.7 to 10.4 weeks

Figure 18

The bonus scoreboard and example payout table (see figure 20) illustrate how one group achieved a level 6 bonus (or 6 percent of pay) in Q1, 8 percent in Q2, and 6 percent in Q3, and then finished the year at a level 5 (or 5 percent of pay). What's nice about a bonus structure like this is the following:

- We are all in the same bonus plan (management too!).

- We will win as a team.

- We will put the rewards close to the behavior that earned the rewards.

- We will not pay out a reward we did not earn.

Here's a test using the bonus scoreboard (figure 19). We are in Q3, and profit year to date is forecast at $550,000. What bonus level are we tracking?

The answer is level 6. We have not quite achieved the $551,640 we need for a level 7 payout. But man, oh man! Can't we find $1,640 lying around somewhere before the end of the quarter? Another level is worth another twenty hours of pay! People perform differently when they see how their actions and decisions influence their rewards. Trust us. They'll find the $1,640—and more.

Small wins add up to big wins. Everybody knows the annual bonus goal is out there, and they have their sights set on it. But they also know that they can only reach the goal by acting on the everyday activities that drive or "move the needle" on the Critical Number.

You've already learned that MiniGames break the Critical Number down into the Right Drivers that make all the difference. It may be a small game and a small reward or recognition, but every small win puts us that much closer to the big win. They are a great way to help people maintain line of sight and engagement from day to day.

Don't forget to always be drawing the connections between these short-term rewards and longer-term rewards. Great MiniGames should drive our Critical Numbers. So winning thirty-, sixty-, and ninety-day rewards in MiniGames should be driving quarterly payouts of the annual bonus plan! Never stop winning!

BONUS SCORECARD EXAMPLE

Hourly	CRITICAL NUMBER (PROFIT BEFORE TAX)				Bonus Plan			
Level	Q1 Target	Q2 Target	Q3 Target	Q4 Target	Bonus Pool	Additional % of pay	Additional days pay	Additional hours pay
Plan	162,500	325,000	487,500	650,000	...	...	...	...
Threshold	150,000	300,000	450,000	600,000	...	...	...	...
1	152,420	307,260	464,520	624,200	12,100	1%	2.6	20.8
2	154,840	314,520	479,040	648,400	24,200	2%	5.2	41.6
3	157,260	321,780	493,560	672,600	36,300	3%	7.8	62.4
4	159,680	329,040	508,080	696,800	48,400	4%	10.4	83.2
5	162,100	336,300	522,600	721,000	60,500	5%	13.0	104.0
6	164,520	343,560	537,120	745,200	72,600	6%	15.6	124.8
7	166,940	350,820	551,640	769,400	84,700	7%	18.2	145.6
8	169,360	358,080	566,160	793,600	96,800	8%	20.8	166.4
9	171,780	365,340	580,680	817,800	108,900	9%	23.4	187.2
10	174,200	372,600	595,200	842,000	121,000	10%	26.0	208.0

(Base Pay x Level % x Progressive Payout%)-(Previous Payout)

Figure 19

BONUS PAYOUT TABLE EXAMPLE

EXAMPLE PAYOUT			$30,000 PROJECTED WAGES	
By Quarter	Q1	Q2	Q3	Q4
Level Achieved	Level 6	Level 8	Level 6	Level 5
% of wages	6%	8%	6%	5%
Projected Annual Payout	$1,800	$2,400	$1,800	$1,500
Progressive Payment	10%	30%	60%	100%
YTD Cash Payout	$180	$720	$1,080	$1,500
Less Payouts Received	$0	$180	$720	$1,080
Quarterly Cash Payout	$180	$540	$360	$420

Figure 20

Communicate, Communicate, Communicate

The most common reason bonus plans fail is poor communication. Your carefully crafted goals and your ingenious payout schedule are worth nothing if people can't follow them, understand them, and buy in to them.

Bonus plan success will have everything to do with how well we communicate and encourage our people to stay in The Game. They need to stay focused on their Critical Number*s,* make sure they're acting on the right financial drivers, and persistently—let's repeat—*persistently* communicate progress by keeping score and following the action day in and day out.

Visit a Great Game practitioner sometime if you want to see our approach to communicating and driving the bonus plan. Scoreboards and the weekly financial Huddles are great ways to keep up the education and energy. We'll describe this entire communication process in the next few chapters. This is where it all comes together. With a regular, company-wide, big-picture review of the business and the financial outlook, employees can not only track the progress of The Game but also forecast their own bonus.

Always Celebrate the Win and Recognize the Players

One of leadership's most valuable tools for accomplishing company goals and improving employees' quality of life is the simple act of recognition—identifying and acknowledging the performance of the team or individuals who have performed above and beyond expectations.

For people to pitch in and really give the challenge their full and immediate attention, they must know, without question, that everybody is in it together and that they will be rewarded and recognized appropriately for their efforts. It's not all about pay, although pay is important. It's about enjoying where you work and knowing you are appreciated for the contributions you make.

That's why The Great Game of Business is very much about rewarding, celebrating, and recognizing players day in and day out.

DESIGN STEPS

Here are some helpful design steps to follow, along with a bonus design tool:

1. Define the Critical Number(s). Companies frequently tie their bonus plans to the Critical Number of profit to ensure that people stay focused on making money. And profits are a reliable and easy way to fund the bonus payouts. In some cases, companies may select an additional Critical Number to be tied to the bonus plan. For example, one GGOB practitioner, a $10 million engineering consulting firm, tied a portion of its bonus to client referrals. For this company, the bonus plan was first based on profit before tax, but client referrals acted as a qualifier to open up the gate to a

full bonus payout. If the client reached its profit targets, 50 percent of the bonus payout was provided for that achievement. The other 50 percent of the payout was dependent on what percent of total revenue was achieved for client referrals.

2. Establish the minimum performance (threshold). Be sure to include all the investments required to maintain the long-term financial security of the company. A healthy company means job security and opportunity.

3. Determine the size of the bonus pool. You'll need to project your total payroll based on the plan you have put together for the coming year. Then, you'll need to decide where you will cap the bonus program, expressed as a percentage of salaries/wages and payroll taxes. For example, with a total payroll of $1 million and a cap of 15 percent of payroll, your total potential bonus pool is $150,000 if the team maxes it out for the year.

4. Decide on how to distribute the pool. By far the most common approach is to distribute a bonus pool as a percentage of an employee's wages. That way, everyone from the front line to the CEO can participate in the same bonus plan—everyone gets the same percentage. (Employees with higher salaries will receive a larger bonus in dollar terms.) This is often the most equitable approach, since in most cases salaries and wages will reflect greater responsibilities and experience. A few organizations prefer to share the available bonus pool by "equal share"; that is, the pool is divided to pay everyone the same dollar amount. Decide which is best for your culture and your team.

5. Determine the payout schedule. In nearly forty years of actual use, the quarterly "10–20–30–40" plan has never failed. We've met a few folks whose teams chose to get fewer (hence bigger) payouts, but that's rare. If you choose another payout schedule, be sure to stress test it repeatedly before rolling it out. And remember, providing early and frequent bonus payouts ties the reward closer to the behaviors that created them.

6. Establish a time for *declaring* and *paying* the bonus. This should be in your plan document, for sure. Set expectations by being realistic about when you can have the books closed and have solid actuals. Remember, we never pay a bonus we haven't earned. You can forecast and declare the bonus payouts, but make sure the team understands when checks will be in hand.

7. Stress test the plan. Modeling the bonus plan is essential. Use our Bonus Plan Modeling Tool as well as different scenarios to make sure your threshold is right, the payouts are motivating, and people believe it's all achievable. Further, does this bonus plan ensure long-term success for your employees and your company?

8. Include administrative issues, and develop a plan document. As much thought as you put into the bonus itself, you should prepare a plan document as well. This is an explanation of the way the plan works and a declaration of the rules governing it. Even though you may not anticipate any problems with team members now, having a plan document will help you avoid issues in the future. Your compensation advisors are the best resources to make sure any bonus plan is right for you.

9. Communicate and educate everyone on the plan. In a vacuum of information, people fill the void with misinformation, assumption, rumor, and gossip. Try to leave no stone unturned; if the plan is hard to understand, it won't motivate. If people can forecast their own bonus after a Huddle, *now you've got 'em!*

10. Celebrate the win. Many people don't wake up feeling like winners. Create a culture of ownership and of winning—at work. If people win more at work, they begin to win more at home. And when they win more at home, they tend to win more in their communities. Don't forget to recognize the players and celebrate the win! Make it memorable.

SHORT-, MID-, AND LONG-TERM REWARDS

Through the years, The Great Game community has proven the power of connecting people with rewards that link the short-, mid-, and long-term goals of the business.

At SRC, we use MiniGames (short-term); the annual bonus plan (midterm); and our ESOP (long-term). The MiniGames focus on drivers to our Critical Number, providing rewards every thirty days. If we are hitting our Critical Number, our annual bonus plan pays out quarterly, and that should be driving the value of our business and our stock price.

Hilcorp in Houston uses a similar approach but adds a five-year incentive program that ensures the value of the company doubles every five years.

PROVIDE A STAKE IN THE OUTCOME: HILCORP

Hilcorp has come a long way since 1989, when the founders described themselves as "three guys and a telephone" trying to make a living.

Today, Hilcorp is one of the largest privately held independent energy exploration and production companies in the United States. The company's meteoric rise is a testament to its unwavering commitment to unleashing the power of human capital. "Early on, I worked at places where bonuses were pennies from heaven," says founder and president Jeff Hildebrand. "Hilcorp ties incentives to things our people can control."

Hildebrand built his company with The Great Game of Business as its foundation, and its ownership culture is second to none. Every day, employees live the company's core values: ownership, integrity, urgency, alignment, and improvement. They don't have "jobs"; they work as owners with purpose and passion.

Through the years, Hilcorp has done a beautiful job tying people's short-term, midterm, and long-term rewards to the goals of the company.

Short-Term Rewards

Competitive salaries and benefits coupled with a strong culture consistently put Hilcorp at the top of lists like Fortune's "Best Companies to Work For" and "Great Places to Work." Hilcorp also uses MiniGames extensively to drive execution toward annual Critical Numbers, plus quarterly payouts of a "share the wealth" bonus plan averaging 34 percent of base salary. This gets people in The Game and keeps them in The Game.

Midterm Rewards

Five-year BHAG (Big Hairy Audacious Goal) megabonuses of up to $100,000 per employee are offered for doubling the company's production, equity, and proved reserves.

Long-Term Rewards

High-quality work life and a clear career path are influenced by a company-wide commitment to doubling the business every five years. In addition, Hilcorp has a unique buy-in program, where employees can put their own money into the projects they work on every day. During the Texas Eagle Ford Shale oil boom, savvy Hilcorp team members saw a twenty-one-times return on their investment.

Hilcorp is also committed to the communities its employees live and work in, so their Stake in the Outcome includes much more than incentives and bonuses and flows into many other aspects of employees' lives.

A Stake in the Outcome is one of the most personal of all the GGOB principles. Hilcorp takes "personal" to the next level. The Hilcorp Helping Hands (HHH) program is an employee-funded-and-managed program that provides a way for their two thousand people to help each other through unusual and unexpected financial hardships, whether it be a death in the family, unusual expenses, or personal losses.

Community is top of mind for everyone, too. Hilcorp establishes a charitable trust for every new employee with an initial gift of $2,500 to be donated at the employee's direction to a charity of their choice.

Hilcorp then matches employee contributions up to $2,000 each year. In addition, there are scholarships and other community investments.

Hildebrand says, "Since we pull together, not competing against each other, and we all have skin in The Game, it's amazing what we can accomplish."

• • •

Bonus plan success will have everything to do with how well you communicate, educate, and encourage your people to stay in The Game and reach for the goal.

Remember, no matter how large the reward, it is often not the only motivating force for many employees. The real motivator is the fact that they are involved and informed—included in discussions about what's going on with the business and what to do about it. They have a trusted, respected seat at the company's decision-making table. And they know through playing The Game that what they say and do really counts.

Download the Bonus Scoreboard Example, Bonus Payout Table Example, Bonus Plan Modeling Tool, and Bonus Plan Communication Tool at www.greatgame.com/gigtools.

1 BEGIN WITH THE RIGHT LEADERSHIP

2 SHARE THE WHY BEFORE THE HOW

3 OPEN THE BOOKS & TEACH THE NUMBERS

4 FOCUS ON THE CRITICAL NUMBER

5 ACT ON THE RIGHT DRIVERS

6 CREATE AN EARLY WIN WITH MINIGAMES

7 PROVIDE A STAKE IN THE OUTCOME

8 **KEEP SCORE**

9 FOLLOW THE ACTION

10 SUSTAIN WITH HIGH-INVOLVEMENT PLANNING

STEP 8

KEEP SCORE

Are we winning or losing?

n sports, we enjoy the game because we can easily follow the action and keep score. By following the action and keeping score, we experience it all—the stories behind the score, what individual actions and team accomplishments changed the score, what plays made the difference, and ultimately how the game was won. Every sport has its scoreboard, scorecards, and team stats—and so must every business.

However, unlike sports, too many businesses are running their companies by focusing their players on the stats and only the stats, all without ever really knowing if they're winning or losing. They have no visibility to the center-court scoreboard (the financials). It goes back to our story about bowling through a curtain. The people who have their hands on the ball and therefore the greatest opportunity to change the score and win the game have no idea where to take aim.

A number of years ago, while on a visit to a *Fortune* 500 company, we were proudly led through its expansive facilities as our guide lauded the extensive scoreboarding that was happening at every turn. Man, they measured *everything*. They had KPIs on safety, utilization, units, employee engagement, and even temperature. In total, they boasted an impressive 157 KPIs they tracked at any given moment.

At the culmination of the tour, the executive beamed with pride when he asked what we thought of all this amazing tracking and measuring. Jack asked him, "So how do you know if you're winning?" Dumbfounded, the exec retorted, "Well, we're winning in some areas and struggling in others," pointing to different scorecards in the meeting room. Stack asked again, "But how do you know if you're winning? Are you making any money?" It seems the *only* thing that wasn't being measured in that incredible operation was if all their efforts were worth it. They weren't watching the ultimate scoreboard—the financials.

Companies that focus only on KPIs can sometimes miss out on larger goals. Is it possible to be profitable and still run out of cash? Is it possible to hit quality goals and still lose a customer? Absolutely. Balancing all the aspects of business simultaneously is imperative, albeit challenging.

SCORING OPPORTUNITIES

Great Game scoreboards inform players if they're winning or losing—and that begins with the financial scoreboard. All the other scoreboards in The Game align to the financials: The Critical Number scoreboard, departmental/team scoreboards, MiniGame scoreboards, and even individual player scorecards. Done well, they all connect (see figure 21), providing a clear line-of-sight for every employee so that they know what they do impacts the overall all score of The Game.

Remember that team scoreboards at any and all levels of the organization should align in such a way that all players can see how they fit—moving the process of keeping score from "them measuring us" to "us measuring ourselves." Keeping score gives winners the critical feedback they need to make the right adjustments, improve performance, and win. This alignment keeps people in The Game feeling that they are contributing to the team toward a common goal—the Critical Number.

SCORING OPPORTUNITIES

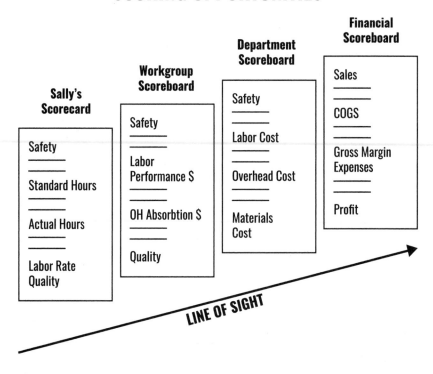

Figure 21

The best place to begin designing your first scoreboard is with the financial scoreboard. We can then begin to align the entire organization to the overall financial performance of the company, rather than randomly choosing measurements that may or may not make an impact. Or worse, pick from a smorgasbord of KPIs you can find on the internet.

FINANCIAL SCOREBOARD

It was 1494 when a Franciscan friar named Luca Pacioli popularized the financial statements like the P&L we use today. But one thing he forgot to include was another column—a column where you can put someone's name: the owner of the line item.

Each person in the business has accountability for those line items you are building. All of a sudden, the financials don't seem like something an accountant dreamed up—they are the facts of everyone's daily life.

Get the Design Team together to discuss the following four important concepts that make Great Game scoreboarding unique and powerful.

Common-Sense Financials

Turn your financial information into a common-sense, simplified scoreboard. The "books" that employees use in The Great Game of Business to manage financial outcomes are not full-scale annual reports. Your financial scoreboard is a simplified version of your financial statements that revolves around the company's Critical Numbers. When we talk about common-sense financials, we mean financials that are unpacked—providing information not just about the whole company or business unit but about individual departments and processes, showing what key measures are needed in order for employees to understand how the financials are created.

Remember, it is not as important to be GAAP (Generally Accepted Accounting Principles) compliant as it is to be clear on where and how the numbers are created.

Bottom-Up Financials

Instead of sharing financials with your employees, try asking your employees to share the numbers with you. With The Great Game of Business, information comes from every corner of the business into an accurate, up-to-the-minute *big-picture* view of the company's financial performance. It starts with the Design Team leading the way. In time, each line item on the financial scoreboard will be owned and represented by a broader group of people as they learn the business.

Real-Time Forward-Looking Financials

You can't change history. We want information in real time, not past time.

Many companies steer their businesses while facing backward. They tend to measure the past, which is telling them only what has happened. The key is spending less time discussing what *has* occurred and more time discussing what *will* happen in the future—and what we can do differently tomorrow to help create a better future. Design your financial scoreboard in a forward-focused format.

Living Financials

The primary purpose of creating real-time common-sense financials is to help bring operational and financial realities to life and make them interesting, understandable, and relevant to everyone in the company. In most companies, it's the responsibility of various managers and financial officers to track, measure, and report the numbers that are used to produce the financial reports. While the above holds true in Great Game companies as well, this reporting responsibility is shared *much more widely*. For example, frontline employees are responsible for tracking, measuring, and reporting their own operational numbers as well as how those numbers impact financial results. These employees are responsible for helping to gather the data that goes into their line items, for forecasting their numbers to the company, and for understanding what's happening to their line items over time.

FINANCIAL SCOREBOARD DESIGN

With the Design Team in the appropriate mind-set, you can now begin designing and using an effective financial scoreboard. Here is a thorough walk-through of a well-designed, company-wide financial scoreboard (see figure 22).

1. Line numbers: Since financial terminology will be new to most employees, you should number each line item so that you can easily direct employees to its location on your scoreboard.

2. Line items: Get the Design Team together and a chart of accounts. Begin to unpack the financials, identifying what numbers will be used and how the numbers will be organized. Every number should be represented, though some may be consolidated, like salaries. A line item may be a sum total of a group of charts of accounts. For example, total sales and marketing expenses may include travel expenses but are simply rolled up in the line item. Each line item may include items that are tracked through additional scorecards that make up this line item. Each scorecard may have additional owners; however, they roll up to the overall line item on the financial scoreboard. For example, a purchase-price variance scorecard would roll up to a material cost line item or a Cost of Goods Sold line item. Try to limit the line items

to those that are most important and represent the greatest impact to the overall scoreboard. Include the 20 percent of accounts that represent 80 percent of the impact. And focus on those line items that employees can influence. If employees have questions regarding items that are within those sum total line items, you can expand that specific item out until people are educated on the number.

3. Calculations column: Include a calculation for each line item so the employees have a "cheat sheet" on how to calculate the score. Be sure to ask your employees to help calculate the score. This ensures that employees pay attention and learn how financial information is calculated. Sometimes you may want to call on employees to calculate the score and provide rewards and recognition for employees that participate. This enables and encourages employees to get involved, which will also help them learn the numbers.

4. Plan: This includes your current year's monthly plan for each line item, which will remain fixed throughout the plan year. This number should come directly from your annual plan. If you have not yet created an annual plan, you could temporarily use your prior year's actual results for each line item. This at least provides a comparison to what has been done before. Providing the previous year's performance gives everyone another benchmark to compare current performance to identify variances.

5. Owner: This identifies the owner—the person primarily accountable for the line item. The line owner is responsible for providing the forecast, but also for knowing the

story behind the number. Since the line must be forecast at every Huddle, it's a best practice to identify a primary and a backup line owner.

6. Forward forecasting: Forecasting is the fundamental way in which GGOB practitioners communicate with the numbers and enable employees to act—and to take responsibility for the financial performance of the company. A forecast is simply a collective best estimate or opinion on what is expected and a commitment to do what we say we are going to do. It's a combination of the actual data available to you (historical data, actual results, benchmarks, leading indicators, etc.), your assumptions (an informed, educated opinion), and what you are committing to the organization to achieve (your goal/commitment). There are five columns under the "Forward Forecasting" heading, which will house each line owners' month-end forecast. A common mistake is thinking that this week's forecast or actuals go here. Nope. This space is reserved for how you think the month will end. Then next week, forecast again how the month will end, and so on. We take a closer look at forecasting in the next chapter.

7. Final: This represents the final results for the month after the books have been closed. There is a lot to learn from comparing final results to the owner's last forecast, especially in the beginning. The finals often include accounting adjustments, like accruals, that are not yet understood by the line owners.

8. Actual YTD and Plan YTD: This represents the actual year-to-date or cumulated performance. These columns provide

a quick year-to-date comparison to plan.

9. Critical Number and Driver Line Items: This section could include line items that represent your Critical Number performance or key Drivers that do not directly appear on your Financial Scoreboard. These could be items from the balance sheet or cash flow statement or ratios like inventory turns. They could be key Drivers to achieving the Critical Number, for example, referrals, billable hours, purchase receipts, net promoter score, accounts receivable, and so on.

Coach's Tip: Provide your employees a list of definitions for each line Item. Remember, this is new to people, so the first time they hear a line item like "reimbursed outside services," there are going to be some puzzled faces around the room. Make it a safe space to learn by providing a guidebook.

Line #	FINANCIAL SCOREBOARD — Line Items (2)	Calculation (3)	PLAN (4)	Owner (5)	FORWARD FORECAST (6) Forecast 1	Forecast 2	Forecast 3	Forecast 4	FINAL (7)	ACTUAL YTD (8)	PLAN YTD
1	**REVENUE**										
2	Product or Customer A		$4,500,000	Joe	$5,000,000	$5,000,000	$5,000,000	$5,000,000	$5,000,000		
3	Product or Customer B		$1,200,000	Sue	$1,200,000	$1,000,000	$1,000,000	$1,200,000	$1,100,000		
4	Total Revenue	2:3 = 4	$5,700,000		$6,200,000	$6,000,000	$6,000,000	$6,200,000	$6,100,000		
5	**COST OF GOODS SOLD**										
6	Materials		$1,000,000	Bill	$1,000,000	$900,000	$900,000	$1,000,000	$950,000		
7	Labor		$1,250,000	Steve	$1,500,000	$1,500,000	$1,500,000	$1,500,000	$1,500,000		
8	Overhead		$1,250,000	Lucy	$1,250,000	$1,250,000	$1,250,000	$1,250,000	$1,250,000		
9	Cost of Goods Sold	6:8 = 9	$3,500,000		$3,750,000	$3,650,000	$3,650,000	$3,750,000	$3,700,000		
10	GROSS MARGIN	4-9 = 10	$2,200,000		$2,450,000	$2,350,000	$2,350,000	$2,450,000	$2,400,000		
11	GM %	10/4 = 11	39%		40%	39%	39%	40%	39%		
12	**EXPENSES**										
13	General & Admin Expenses		500,000	Mary	500,000	500,000	500,000	500,000	500,000		
14	Sales & Marketing Expenses		700,000	Rick	750,000	750,000	750,000	750,000	750,000		
15	Facility Expenses		450,000	Philip	450,000	450,000	450,000	450,000	420,000		
16	Total Expenses	13:15 = 16	1,650,000		1,700,000	1,700,000	1,700,000	1,700,000	1,645,000		
17	**PROFIT BEFORE TAX**	10-16 = 17	**550,000**		**750,000**	**650,000**	**650,000**	**750,000**	**755,000**		
18	PBT %	17/4 = 18	10%		12%	11%	11%	12%	12%		
19	**OTHER CRITICAL NUMBERS & DRIVERS**										
20	Net Promoter Score		60	Julie	60	60	60	60	65		
21	Client Referrals	(9)	10	Sue	10	10	8	8	9		
22	A/R over 30 days		$10,000	Brian	$5,000	$5,000	$5,000	$5,000	$4,000		

Figure 22

143

KEEPING SCORE: PACIFIC OUTDOOR LIVING

Sometimes practitioners of The Game take GGOB ideas like score-boarding to another level of execution. A few years ago during a visit to Los Angeles, we stopped in to say hello to Terry Morrill. He and his family own Pacific Outdoor Living (POL), Southern California's leading designer and installer of high-end landscapes and aquascapes.

When you walk through their headquarters, it looks nothing like a landscaping business might look. The walls and offices are lined with scoreboards that track every key measurable you can imagine. From a master scheduling board down to an individual scorecard above someone's computer, you can actually see the line of sight and connection to the Critical Number—both for individuals and the team. Pacific Outdoor Living is great example of how the chain of scoreboards, bottom to top and top to bottom, allow information to flow up, down, and across the organization. Years ago, Pacific Outdoor Living introduced The Great Game to apply financial rigor to its existing employee empowerment systems.

"The Great Game got us to critically review our key stats to ensure they directly contribute to our bottom line," explains administrator Athena Owen. "It really helped us to minimize confusion and increase production." Great Game of Business also created a new understanding for employees. Instead of just tracking KPIs and metrics, they now connect all measures with the ultimate "score" of whether we are winning or losing—the financials.

Supervisors meet for morning Huddles to discuss projects and adjust forecasts. And the fifteen work crews participate in a Huddle weekly to calculate their own forecasts and post them on the company-wide Game board.

Terry's commitment to ongoing training has led to higher levels of both team participation and personal responsibility for producing superior work. Not to mention world-class growth, Pacific Outdoor Living has been recognized as one of the fastest-growing companies in America. That means more jobs and better careers, if you're keeping score. Employees continue to take high-level, entrepreneurial-management courses that teach them how to analyze financial statements and to calculate breakeven—a measure they use daily to make profit-minded decisions.

• • •

Although the practice of business scorecards and dashboards has become very popular in recent years, it has been estimated that more than half of all scorecard and dashboard projects have failed to provide any positive business results. Why do they continually fall short on driving results? Many times, it's simply because no one is openly discussing the wins and the losses. In short, there is a lack of effective communication around the scoreboards and a lack of commitment to holding each other accountable.

While Great Game scoreboards will help us clearly determine if we are winning or losing and who's accountable, the Huddle becomes the catalyst for action and holding each other accountable for results.

Download Company-Wide Financial Scoreboard and other Scoreboard examples at www.greatgame.com/gigtools.

1 — BEGIN WITH THE RIGHT LEADERSHIP

2 — SHARE THE WHY BEFORE THE HOW

3 — OPEN THE BOOKS & TEACH THE NUMBERS

4 — FOCUS ON THE CRITICAL NUMBER

5 — ACT ON THE RIGHT DRIVERS

6 — CREATE AN EARLY WIN WITH MINIGAMES

7 — PROVIDE A STAKE IN THE OUTCOME

8 — KEEP SCORE

9 — **FOLLOW THE ACTION**

10 — SUSTAIN WITH HIGH-INVOLVEMENT PLANNING

FOLLOW THE ACTION— HUDDLES AND FORWARD FORECASTING

**Develop a communication rhythm, and hold
each other accountable for results.**

The Great Game needs active players, not bench sitters. We need to empower our people to take an active role; they need to be ready to learn, ready to participate, ready to take responsibility, and ready to stretch for the goal. People get involved when they see themselves in the big picture. The best approach to doing this is to show them frequently how they are all invested in The Game—from the long-term financial success of the company to their personal Stake in the Outcome. We do all this in a Huddle.

FOLLOW THE ACTION—JENNER AG

Nothing can duplicate the kind of informal practical learning that comes with keeping score and following the numbers day in and day out. That's the power of having a consistent Huddle rhythm. But the team at Jenner Ag, the Case IH agriculture-application equipment distributor for the states of Illinois and Indiana, has taken the art of huddling and training to another level when it comes to teaching its eighty-three associates how to think and act like owners.

For what it's worth, the company hasn't missed or cancelled a Huddle since it started playing The Game in 2011.

Under the leadership of CEO Steve Jones, Jenner Ag uses its weekly departmental and forecasting Huddles as well as its monthly company-wide Huddles as opportunities to connect the lessons associates learn in more formal financial literacy classes—what Jenner Ag calls "boot camps"—with how the business actually works. They use their Huddles to connect the day-to-day actions of the associates to create a line of sight into how those actions impact the company.

Jones admits that keeping The Game fresh over the long haul can be a challenge—especially when it comes to making financial literacy training engaging to his associates. "There are only so many times you can explain retained earnings," he says.

That's why Jenner Ag began adding new components to its departmental and company-wide Huddles over the years to keep things interesting. One particularly novel addition it has made is to assign a business or personal financial literacy topic to an associate each Huddle. That associate then gives a five-to-seven-minute report on the assigned topic during the Huddle. "We've asked our people to do something that ninety percent of the general public fears the most," says Jones. "Public speaking. But by creating safe zones in our

Huddles where people could stand up in a supportive environment, we saw a way to use The Game to blend in personal elements along with financial and industry knowledge. One thing I hear consistently from the associates is that they are thankful for the education they get at this company."

The topics the team has covered during Huddles include educating associates on subjects within their industry, answering questions like, "How far apart should corn rows be planted?" "What happens to corn after it leaves an elevator?" And even, "What the heck is NAFTA?"

The team has also tackled a wide variety of personal finance subjects, such as, "How much life insurance do you need?" "What is the impact of underinflated tires?" And "What is a credit score?"

"We believe that people learn best by teaching," says Clint Hohenstein, Jenner Ag's CFO. "Learning about these topics and then teaching others about them is an opportunity for our associates to get outside of their box."

Since the company operates out of three locations across two states, it records its Huddles so that anyone can access the content at a later date. The company also records its monthly company meetings, which are mandatory to attend if associates want to participate in the company's Stake in the Outcome bonus program.

It has also added a competitive element to its company Huddles. They use a web-based app called Kahoot, which is kind of like a quiz show that lets you create your own questions. The associates then break into teams and compete to answer questions based on the company financial information or other topical information that was shared in the departmental Huddles. "It's another way we keep reinforcing what we are teaching while keeping it fresh in everyone's mind," says Autumn Pitman of Jenner Ag's Recruiting and Retention department. "No one can say they don't know something, because we have it out there in a million different ways."

All Jenner Ag associates also get what is called a "player stat," which is a quarterly objective measurement of their individual goals they established at the beginning of the year with their supervisor. The progress on the player stats are then posted at every Huddle as a way for all associates to know if they are tracking toward their goals—or not. Similarly, since the stats are made public, everyone in the company can measure the progress of everyone else—which eliminates any surprises at the end of the quarter. "It also gives us the opportunity to help out if someone is struggling along the way," says Pitman. "Our goal is to work together as one, since we will win or lose as a team."

As Jack O'Riley, Jenner Ag's Great Game coach, puts it, "At Jenner Ag, playing The Game is not a spectator sport. You can't watch it—you have to play."

• • •

Successful practitioners frequently tell us that the moment they were *convinced* The Game was exactly what they needed was their first visit to a Great Game Huddle. It's mind blowing for first-timers to see an entire organization come together to calculate the financial score in real time, one line item, one story, one commitment at a time.

If companies are playing The Game well, you should be able to walk into their Huddles and tell if they are winning or losing—without knowing a single thing about what they do.

You can see and feel the engagement, the ownership, the pride in the room, the values they stand for. You can experience all of that by simply attending a Huddle. That's the beauty of it. In less than forty-five minutes, everyone in the organization is linked up to the big picture.

In this chapter, you'll learn about what a Huddle is, the compo-

ɔf a Huddle Cycle, the non-negotiables of good Huddle design, and tips on conducting a great Huddle of your own.

WHAT'S A HUDDLE?

Great Game Huddles provide a communication rhythm where everyone is kept informed, involved, and engaged in the progress of The Game.

The Huddle is the convergence of the entire Great Game process. This is where it all comes together. This is where all the principles and practices of The Game come to life by exchanging information up, down, and across the organization. The Huddle is our weekly ritual of forecasting the score. It's where we learn how we are progressing toward our Critical Number and how we are tracking to a bonus payout. This is where we share our wins and losses and celebrate our latest MiniGame. This is where we share the numbers, teach each other the business, and see the results of our education.

This is where we see if all our actions and decisions are making a difference. "Are we making money? If not, what's the next play?" It's where The Game becomes real.

> *Our Huddles are the focal point for everything we do—our Huddles directly reflect how well we are playing, week in, week out. This is where we put into practice all of the principles of The Game and reinforce our culture, regenerate the pride and the sense of ownership, how we create mutual trust and respect, build credibility, light the fire in people's eyes.*
>
> *—Jack Stack,* The Great Game of Business

Most people we meet think our Huddles consist of one big "all team" Huddle where financial information is gathered and shared. However, it's what happens *before and after* the main Huddle that really makes the difference. Done well, the Huddle process is all-inclusive. It involves the janitor you hired last week to the chief executive officer. In a Great Game Huddle, employees frequently track progress, commit to results, and continually think about how they could improve those results. *Great Huddles should draw people into the action.* In The Great Game, people aren't just handed the numbers. They help *produce* the numbers by tracking and reporting their work group or department performance. Because they have a common goal (bottom-line financial results) and are working from a common scoreboard, they easily collaborate between departments, focusing their energies on the critical issues of the business. And because they openly discuss wins and losses, they keep learning and getting better. We do all this through a Huddle Cycle.

THE HUDDLE CYCLE

In the Huddle Cycle, numbers are created and shared at a series of Huddles from daily departmental team check-ins (Pre- and Post-Huddles) to weekly company-wide gatherings (the Main Huddle). Information comes from every corner of the business into an accurate, up-to-the-minute, big-picture view of the company's overall financial performance.

The Huddle Cycle includes three types of Huddles (see figure 23):

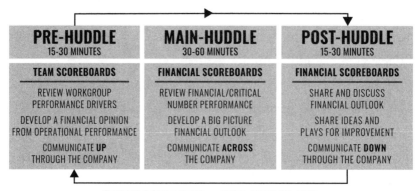

Figure 23

The Pre-Huddle

The Pre-Huddle is the first of the three Huddles in the Huddle Cycle. The primary scoreboard used in this Huddle is the Team Scoreboard.

Typical organizations have frequent operations meetings that bring KPIs and metrics *down* to the front line, with the leader stating, "Here's what we need to do today/this week." Great Game companies are not typical; in Pre-Huddles, we flip the script.

In the Pre-Huddle, team members review their work-group performance, develop a financial opinion (or forecast), and communicate the information *up* through the company. As we described in "Keep Score," each department or team has created a scoreboard that reflects the Critical Numbers and key drivers for their respective areas. In the Pre-Huddle, these leading operational indicators of financial results are tracked, measured, and discussed. The teams then use this information to develop an updated financial forecast.

For example, the sales department's daily and weekly review

of their lead measures (e.g., qualified contacts, closure rates, and submitted proposals) will provide insight into forecast revenue for the month. The production department's review (e.g., direct labor hours, overtime, and rework) will provide a clear opinion of cost of goods sold for the month.

Pre-Huddles are designed to make the connection between operational performance and financial performance. Making this connection helps everyone begin to understand what they can do, both individually and as a team, to impact financial outcomes.

*Pre-Huddles communicate the numbers and the stories behind the numbers **up** through the company.*

Pre-Huddle Basics

- Who attends?

  □ Functional departments or cross-departmental teams. Every person in your company should be attending at least one Pre-Huddle.

- When?

  □ Weekly forecasting, supplemented by daily operational check-ins.

- What length of time?

  □ Fifteen to thirty minutes. Keep them frequent, swift, and on time.

- Who runs it?

  □ The senior manager of the particular team or team leaders.

- What's the focus?

    □ Gathering information and preparing for the Main Huddle.

- Where does it take place?

    □ Almost anywhere. It can be done in person, over the phone, or via videoconference.

The Main Huddle

The Main Huddle is the second of the three Huddles in the Huddle Cycle. The primary scoreboard used in this Huddle is the Financial Scoreboard. In this Huddle, functional departments or teams review financial performance and the company's Critical Number(s), develop a big-picture financial outlook (or forecast), and communicate it *across* the entire organization.

In The Great Game of Business, we communicate through the language of business—the financials. The financials are the only report card in the company that show the collective contribution of each and every department and individual in the enterprise. So, why not use them to bring people together?

The Main Huddle provides a company-wide, big-picture review of the business and its financial outlook. Each employee and each team can clearly see how they impact the big picture, depend on each other, and account for their actions.

*The Main Huddle sends the numbers and the stories behind the numbers **across** the company.*

Main Huddle Basics

- Who attends?
  - Every person in your company should be attending the Main Huddle whenever possible.

- What length of time?
  - Thirty to sixty minutes. Keep them frequent, swift, and on time.

- Who runs it?
  - In most cases, the top leader will run the Main Huddle. However, Huddle leadership can also be rotated among the members of the team, which is a great opportunity to mix it up and give folks "visibility."

- What's the focus?
  - Sharing information and the big picture by providing a forward-focused view of financial and business performance.

- Where does it take place?
  - Likely in your largest gathering space for the on-site team. Be sure to make it available by phone and video-conference for those working off-site.

The Post-Huddle

The Post-Huddle is the last of the three Huddles in the Huddle Cycle. The primary scoreboard used in this Huddle is the Financial Scoreboard. In this Huddle, individual work groups and teams take action on the information they learned in the Main Huddle and call the next plays for improvements, communicating *down* through the company.

It's not company leaders barking out orders after a tough management meeting. It's the front line of the company coming up with ideas and actions to make things better—while they still have time to do it. Because they're thinking in the future by forecasting, they still have time to act.

This is when everyone can apply the big picture in their day-to-day jobs.

If they're $5,000 off their next level of bonus payout, you'd be amazed at how creative people become to find that five grand.

We love the stories we hear from the community about when people "get it." When the lights come on and people shift from a passive role of just doing a job to an active role of making things happen is when you see meaningful change take place. After all, who knows the job better than the person doing the job?

*Post-Huddles communicate the numbers and the stories behind the numbers **down** through the company.*

Post-Huddle Basics

- Who attends?
    - Functional departments or cross-departmental teams. Every person in your company should be attending a Post-Huddle.

- What length of time?
    - Fifteen to thirty minutes. Keep them frequent, swift, and on time.

- Who runs it?
    - The senior manager of the particular team or team leaders.

- What's the focus?
    - Acting on information by planning and running the next play.
    - The Post-Huddle provides an ideal forum to discuss ideas for improvements, the specific needs of the team, and the "one thing" the team can do to improve the score.
- Where does it take place?
    - Like the Pre-Huddle, it can be done in person, over the phone, or via videoconference.

Coach's Tip: Small organizations often have a two-stage Huddle Cycle—the Pre-Huddle and the Main Huddle (see figure 24). In other words, individuals prepare their line items for the Main Huddle, and then, while building the financials together, they can also make their commitments for how they will change the score in the coming week—all in the context of the Main Huddle. Then they run the plays. The feedback loop continues ...

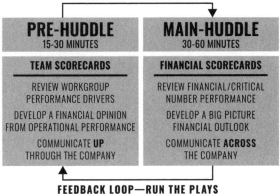

Figure 24

In the days following the Post-Huddle, teams take action, run the plays, and the cycle continues. The Huddle Cycle is an incredibly effective feedback loop that efficiently brings the numbers and the stories behind the numbers *up* through the company, *across* the company, and *down* through the company. It focuses everyone on the most important goals of the organization—all in a forward-looking manner.

Developing your Huddle Cycle will take effort and patience, but it's worth it. And it doesn't have to be daunting. Before you roll it out to the entire workforce, we suggest you start with your Design Team. Have them model the way. The first month or so will be awkward, unorganized, and longer than expected—in all reality, just plain ugly. But it will become easier (and the forecasts more accurate) as the team figures it out. When leaders show their commitment to the process, it trickles down. Once the Design Team is comfortable with the process and confident with the numbers, they'll be ready to coach others. Gradually add more layers—and players—to the Huddle.

THE HUDDLE AGENDA: THE NON-NEGOTIABLES OF HUDDLE DESIGN

While the concept sounds easy enough, the Huddle must be carefully planned and executed in order to be both effective and efficient. Because of the changing work landscape (NextGen workforce, commuters, multilocation business units, diverse company cultures, etc.), the Huddle is the one aspect of The Great Game of Business that companies have to modify most.

Regardless of how you modify the overall flow of your company Huddle, there are four *non-negotiables* to cover to reconnect, refocus, recommit, and reengage the team.

Evaluate Game Conditions

Reconnect the team to the big picture. When the members of an athletic team huddle up, the first thing they do is realign to the goal and discuss what's happening out on the field—what's working, what isn't. Ensure that everyone in your Huddle is informed about the current company landscape. The Huddle leader should open by giving the team context, perspective, or a theme to follow while going through the numbers. This is a perfect time to share where the company is headed—threats, opportunities, and progress on its goals. People want to feel *connected*. Huddles keep everyone in the loop, up to date, and in touch with whatever is happening in the business.

Maintaining that communication link helps employees feel like part of a team. A good Huddle provides everyone the big picture and their role in it, creating a *connection* to what they do every day and the financial health of the company.

Check the Score

Refocus the team on the most important goals of the company. Now the team is reconnected; time to communicate the company's Critical Numbers and the stories behind the numbers. Highlight and openly discuss wins and losses. Encourage everyone to remain forward focused. Take time to succinctly update the company scoreboard with your team and discuss the results. Warning: Resist the urge to focus on historical financials. You can't do much about history. You *can*, however, use that information to make accurate assumptions on where you will end the month. Stay focused on emerging issues rather than dwelling on the past. The purpose of the Huddle is to *proactively* manage the financial performance of the company and meet or exceed your plans. *Be forward looking.* Focus your discussions on where you plan to be, not where you have been.

We call this practice *forward forecasting*. Don't just report the past—use the numbers to influence the future. Forward forecasting is the fundamental way we communicate the numbers in The Great Game of Business. We encourage people to practice the eighty/twenty rule: 80 percent of our Huddle discussions should be focused on the future and only 20 percent on where we have been and why. Huddles should encourage people to think ahead about what they can do to affect results—how they can influence the numbers rather than just passively share results to date. We will spend more time explaining this process shortly.

While this portion of your Huddle should be fairly succinct (individuals should come to the Huddle prepared and ready to forecast their numbers), do be sure you take time to ensure everyone on the team understands why the numbers are what they are and what that means for the company.

GETTING TO THE STORIES BEHIND THE NUMBERS

Numbers are nothing more than stories about people.

—Jack Stack, The Great Game of Business

Behind every number on the financial statements are hundreds of stories illustrating the many challenges, undertakings, efforts, twists, and turns people went through to accomplish the end number. In learning the stories behind the numbers, your people will begin to learn what must be done to impact the outcome—

whether it affects the production line or the front office. With The Great Game of Business, companies communicate with a focus on turning the numbers into useful, actionable information—knowledge that can be used to make better decisions in the best interest of the company. This can only be accomplished through sharing the stories behind the numbers.

What are some potential stories behind these numbers?

NUMBERS (DATA)	STORIES (INFORMATION)
Revenue is $1,200,000.	Revenue is $1,200,000, which is an increase of 8 percent over the prior year, and is $50,000 over our last forecast ... If we get the production material we are needing, we could see another $25,000 in shipments this month.
Freight expense is $13,000.	Why $13,000? That's 8 percent of sales. Our freight expense is out of control. Our freight last year was less than $5,000. The industry average is 3 percent ... Here is what I think is happening ... What are your thoughts?
A/R is $500,000.	What story could be behind these numbers?
Employee turnover is 12 percent.	What story could be behind these numbers?

Figure 25

To get to the stories behind the numbers, try communicating the numbers with a focus on explaining variances, comparisons to benchmarks, trends, and relationships between the numbers or all-time records. Your stories should include successes as well as failures. We all can learn from both.

Plan the Next Play

Recommit the team to improving the score. With team members aligned and focused, let's concentrate on how they can contribute to the company's success in the coming days. Address any financial deviations, and allow the team to troubleshoot ways (outside of the Huddle, of course) to get back on track. You should keep it focused on problem *identification*, not problem *solving*. If there's a problem that can't be solved with a brief suggestion by the team, then take it off-line.

By taking some time to discuss what's around the corner, you'll create alignment among the team members and foster an environment where everyone is able to independently consider their impact as well as create opportunities to improve the score. Identify any deviations from your plans, and help each other clear the path so that the team can improve on them. Make sure the players have what they need to successfully run the next play. Next, press the team to *recommit* to improving the score by asking the question, *"What is the one thing I can do this week to improve the score?"*

Get Fired Up

Reengage the team by recognizing and celebrating progress through every win—big or small. This is the element that will truly set your Huddle apart from other business meetings. If your intention is to have everyone working together as a team, you *must* take some time to get the team fired up.

This doesn't mean you need to high-five every associate as they exit the meeting or pour a cooler of ice water over a manager's head after a big win (though your employees might get a kick out of such antics). You should, however, take time in your Huddle to highlight personal and team wins.

This includes supporting members of the team who have made life accomplishments such as earning a college degree, participating in a half marathon, or adding a new member to the family. This is your opportunity to show your associates that you value them not only for what they do but also for who they are.

Higher Law of Business #9: If nobody pays attention, people stop caring. People must be seen, heard, and recognized. It doesn't matter if you are winning or losing—if people go to battle every day and no one notices, people will stop caring. Huddles tell people we care. Huddles send a message out every week that we care and want to know how people are progressing and how they are making a difference.

Of course, you can—and should—celebrate team wins and milestones such as signing a new client, earning a bonus, or hitting a workplace safety record.

Remember, the achievements you recognize and celebrate will typically get repeated. If you want to drive positive behavior, you must also recognize it—even by simply taking a moment to cheer and applaud during your Huddle.

Take time to highlight individual and team accomplishments. People want to be recognized. We all appreciate a thank-you every now and then. Celebrating the best from the past twenty-four hours (in the form of wins, good news, personal recognition) is crucial to maintaining a connected team. The timeliness of the Huddle provides an opportunity to recognize the unsung heroes critical to the business's success close to the time the performance has occurred.

For example, during SRC Electrical's Huddle, an exuberant associate named Kim shouts out weekly "U-R-AWESOME" awards— provoking laughs, smiles, and appreciation. Our friends at Amy's Ice Creams have another take on Jack Stack's slogan, "Skip the praise; give us the raise." Amy's found that with a millennial workforce, you have to do both. Its revised slogan is "Start with praise, and follow up with the raise."

Nothing fires up players more than being recognized and appreciated for a job well done—or a game well played.

Again, your company Huddle should be formatted to fit the culture and landscape of your company. However, in the spirit of effectiveness and efficiency, be certain that your Huddles always evaluate game conditions, check the score, plan the next play, and get people fired up. That way, you can be sure you'll have communication, clarity, alignment, and accountability—coupled with a strong sense of urgency to improve the score.

FORWARD FORECASTING: THE FUNDAMENTAL WAY WE COMMUNICATE THE NUMBERS

In The Great Game of Business, forward forecasting is the fundamental way we communicate the numbers, because we want to control our own destiny. Many refer to their GGOB Huddle as a Forecasting Huddle. These Forecasting Huddles are a significant departure from the KPI-driven scorecards you see at many businesses.

Ultimately, Huddles should help us *proactively* manage our performance and the financial results we are after. Some believe that financials are lagging measures and have no use in daily or weekly performance management. However, we use them as our early-warning system.

Imagine that the fire marshal just walked into your office and gave you a message that you never want to hear: your house has just burned to the ground. What would you do? There's not much you can do but sift through the ashes and decide to rebuild or relocate. Now, imagine that same fire marshal walks in and tells you that in *two hours* your house is going to catch fire. What would you do? You'd take action! You'd stop the fire at its source, if possible, or if not, you'd make sure the damage was minimized. It's a completely different conversation, isn't it?

Sometimes, we don't like the message the scoreboard has to tell us, but at least we've got that "two-hour notice." Ignoring the message or not taking it seriously would eventually leave us sifting through ashes. It's not too late to save the house or at the very least minimize the damage. We just have to plan the next play accordingly.

Financial forecasting in business can be very challenging, but the benefits to the short- and long-term health of the organization can be tremendous.

Why forecast?

- Forecasting helps eliminate surprises. In business, no one likes surprises!

- Forecasting ensures we remain proactive so we don't have to wait until the end of the month to learn how we did. We want to impact the outcome while there's still time to make a difference.

- Forecasting encourages employees to think about cause and effect—that is, how they can influence the numbers rather than just passively looking at results to date.

- Forecasting makes us smarter about the business. The ability to predict or forecast accurately is a direct indication of how well people understand their numbers.

- Forecasting creates a sense of urgency, encouraging people to act and take responsibility for improving the score.

How Do You Get Better at Forecasting? Repetition, Repetition, Repetition!

When you start regular Huddles and ask nonfinancial people for an opinion on how the month will end, you're bound to hear, "How am I supposed to predict the future? What am I, a fortune teller?" It's imperative that you teach people that "it's not your job to *predict* the future. Your job is to *influence* it." We'll never be able to see around every corner, but with each forecast, we get a little smarter. A little more accurate. We seek out more information; we ask more sources. While we might call it "poorcasting" in the beginning, it's the discipline of keeping at it week after week, month after month, that makes us better. At SRC, our monthly forecasts have proven 95 percent accurate. In fact, our most recent five-year financial forecasts proved to be 96 percent accurate. Sound impossible? Believe it—you will get better. Just keep at it. In business, we don't like things sneaking up on us. So, forecasting helps us take the surprises out of business.

We are not asking people to predict the unpredictable. We are simply asking them to be forward looking and then learn what impacts their numbers. Their forecast is simply an educated best estimate or opinion on what is expected.

> *Your forecast is your commitment to the organization. It's not something you throw out and hope happens. It's your near-term vision. If you have doubts, go communicate, talk it out, and take action; that's how you beat the conditions.*

—Jack Stack

In the end, forecasting will help you gain a deeper understanding of what influences your numbers. Begin by identifying the few key drivers that directly influence your forecast. For example, a sales team is responsible for sales revenue, so the key drivers that may directly influence its forecast are number of customer prospects, closure rate, number of proposals submitted, product mix, revenue per customer, customer satisfaction, sales cycle, new business, and average sale price.

Here's how the process works.

Part of the "secret sauce" in playing The Great Game of Business is developing a consistent Huddle rhythm that includes forward forecasting your financial scoreboard by line owners—those people close to the numbers who have responsibility for reporting each line of the scoreboard.

Refer back to the financial scoreboard in Step 8 (see figure 22). The scoreboard is not a financial statement—rather, it's a common-sense *reflection* of your income statement, balance sheet, and cash flow statements. Your financial scoreboard should include important data that your team wants and needs to know.

During your Huddle, you'll be keeping score on a number of scoreboards (bonus plan, MiniGames, etc.), but start with the financial scoreboard.

Begin by having the sales team call out its revenue forecast for the end of the month. If you're at the beginning of the month, this forecast will go in the "Forecast 1" column. Then you can work your way down the scoreboard, quickly capturing forecasts of how the month will end from people who own lines relating to COGS and expenses. Remember to ask for the stories behind the numbers, especially if there is a variance from the plan. Our rule of thumb is that if you are above or below plan by 5 percent to 10 percent, you must tell a quick story, explaining the deviation.

In a matter of minutes, you'll have built a financial picture of how your company will look in the coming weeks. And your team has an understanding of why it will look that way. Employees can now go and take action to mitigate the negatives and lock in the positives.

The following week, you'll repeat the process but with additional data and information available. Data + Assumption x Frequency = Accuracy. Your "Forecast 2" column should look different, as will "Forecast 3" and "Forecast 4" in subsequent Huddles. The key is that we are looking ahead instead of looking back, always with an eye on improving our month-end results.

When you reach the month's end, you'll cover two months in one Huddle. You'll cover the month you're wrapping up plus "Forecast 1" of the upcoming month. In this transitional Huddle, you can reconcile your actuals with your forecast very rapidly. You've been looking at these numbers for four weeks now, so you can take a quick look back and then immediately throw your attention forward again.

FORECASTING BRINGS THE BONUS PLAN TO LIFE

Huddle participants begin to realize that what they do behind the line items on the financial scoreboard has everything to do with what they take home in terms of job security and rewards. Huddles provide a weekly check-in on how people are tracking to their bonus payout. The bonus plan keeps everyone excited, because the stakes rise at every Huddle, every forecast, every month. Remember how the bonus plan is designed. We're always in the bonus hunt, and the rewards become greater each quarter. The prospect of sharing in the financial success of the business makes the pursuit of improvements just a little bit sweeter.

FORWARD FORECASTING: WATCH OUT FOR WEASEL WORDS

At first, embracing the practice of forward forecasting varies across Huddle team members—some take it very seriously while others devote little or no time to this critical process. Longtime GGOB coach Jack O'Riley has been a part of thousands of Huddles. He's seen it all and has learned what to listen for to get everyone on board and effective with forward forecasting. His first advice is not to overthink it. Don't overcomplicate the process. Oh sure, you can use complex Excel spreadsheets drawing upon models such as linear regression or some modeling theory like the Monte Carlo method. Or you can simply draw upon your knowledge of the business, a little historical information, and your experience and intuition and apply all that to the numbers. O'Riley also suggests that when you hear phrases like the following, it should alert you to dig a little deeper and ask questions of the line owner about the forecast.

- **"I am trying to be conservative."**
  This is natural for businesspeople—but not helpful. We want to use all the knowledge available to forecast financials accurately. "Conservative" is not helpful.

- **"This is how much we have booked this month to date."**
  If it is the last day of the month, this is fine. However, if half the month is yet to happen, then using month-to-date data will probably not prove to be accurate.

- **"I am being optimistic."**

  This is as bad as being conservative. We are not looking for optimistic, pessimistic, or conservative. We are looking for what is likely to happen.

- **"I am going on last month's results."**

  Fine, if this month will be like last month. Not fine if this is used as a shortcut to a forecast. "Just use my number from last month" is probably only good if you are forecasting something like rent.

- **"Just use my number from last week."**

  This sets off all sorts of alarms for a coach. Did the line owner even bother to look at the forecast for this Huddle?

- **"I did not have time to look at my numbers."**

  Just not acceptable—this undermines the whole process. If this recurs, this person should not be part of the process.

- **"Just use the plan number."**

  If the plan is new, then using those numbers might be appropriate. If the plan is ten months old, then defaulting to plan numbers is probably not acceptable.

- **"This is my best guess for now until I hear from Tom."**

  Tom does not own the line and the associated forecast. The line owner does.

- **"I am waiting on accounting to get back to me."**

  Accounting is a critical source of information but is not responsible for the forecast. The line owners need to figure out another way to forecast with the data they have for a Huddle.

This list is not exhaustive, but it's a good representation of phrases you need to be on the lookout for in your Huddles. Other "weasel words" that indicate the person doing the forecast is trying to sidestep the responsibility and accountability include words like *nearly*. If you hear phrases like these too often, your Huddle will sort of and nearly be useless.

• • •

STOP MEETING—START HUDDLING

While keeping score with a series of scoreboards helps us clearly determine if we are winning or losing, following the action through a series of Huddles becomes the catalyst for truly effective communication. Following the Action helps an organization close the feedback loop and reconnect, refocus, reengage, and recommit to the success of the company.

HUDDLE TIPS

The tips below will ensure your Huddles are most productive:

Begin with the Right Leadership

Be sure the Huddle lives up to its purpose of helping to consistently inform, involve, engage, educate, and, of course, hold people accountable for the success of the business. Remember, Huddle leaders, that Huddles are for the team, not for the managers.

Focus on the Right Scoreboard

Huddles start with a relevant and meaningful scoreboard, highlighting the right measures that clearly tell the team if they are winning or losing and who's accountable.

Keep Your Huddles Frequent, Swift, and On Time

Maintain a simple, fixed agenda while making sure the content is relevant and the communication is concise and swift. Same day, same time, same place—every week. That way people can count on it. They can plan for it. They can develop a routine around it.

Push Back on the Pushback

The immediate pushback you will get when recommending a frequent Huddle is, "We're too busy!" Executives can't imagine finding the time to get everybody in the same place every week for one minute, let alone thirty to sixty. Yet this discipline will actually save you time. Teams that Huddle frequently find they interrupt each other considerably less and that productivity improves. They understand there is a fixed time when they'll have everyone else's attention.

Assign Employees to Small Teams

In your company-wide Main Huddles, create groups with a manager acting as the team captain to teach and coach the team during the Huddle. The small groups provide a comfortable setting for employees to get involved, ask questions, and provide input—all the things you want the Huddle process to create.

Provide a Blank Scoreboard, and Populate It in Real Time

Give employees a blank scorecard each month to fill out so each can track, measure, and report information during each weekly Huddle. The simple act of writing the numbers down and doing a little math keeps everyone engaged and involved and has a dramatic effect on the employees' ability to learn, understand, and remember how the numbers work together. Try it—it works.

Consider Binders

In an age of electronics, paper seems counterintuitive. But object permanence is a real thing. Consider providing Game binders to the employees that include all the GGOB information they need in order to follow the progress of The Game, including the annual business plan, Huddle scoreboards, bonus plan, a business/financial glossary of terms, training bites, and so on. Think of it as your employees' mobile office—a central place to store all the information they need to follow the action of The Game.

Make It Interesting ... and a Little Fun!

Provide small incentives to employees or their teams to answer questions or make the calculations on the scoreboard. Include small games or brief training bites to reinforce your financial and business literacy efforts. One practitioner created Company-opoly—a customized version of the classic Monopoly game—to begin teaching the balance sheet to its teams.

Encourage Learning

The Huddle should educate people on the business. Highlight the topics that are relevant and useful to the team. Ultimately, people want to know how they can make a difference. It's important to always provide line of sight by making a connection between what they do every day—both individually and as a team—and the financial outcomes of the business.

Keep in Touch with Your Strategic (High-Involvement) Plan

People support what they help create, remember? The more input you get from your team as you put your annual plan together, the more you'll want to reconnect to it during your Huddles. But don't just present numbers. Start a discussion about how the numbers they're forecasting compare to the goals they previously set.

Employees, Not Accounting, Should Generate the Numbers

Employees' efforts created those numbers, so they should be the ones to gather them. This also allows the employees to discover and understand exactly where these numbers are coming from and how their daily efforts drive those numbers.

And They Should Report the Numbers, Too

Give your employees a voice by letting them call out their own forecasts. This allows them to celebrate their successes and mourn their failures with the rest of the company. It's such a great reminder that you're all in it together.

Proactively Highlight People Creating "Stories behind the Numbers"

Your company's success didn't happen magically. There are real, flesh-and-blood people behind everything you do. Show your employees how each one of them plays a role in the company's success by proactively seeking out stories about how the numbers were achieved. This adds an extra layer of accountability and ownership.

Always Keep It High Energy

Don't be like Ferris Bueller's economics teacher, droning your audience into submission. Bring the energy. Your employees aren't going to get excited if you aren't engaged in the process. Ask questions. Give out kudos. Show your passion for making the company a great place for everyone to work and achieve success. Remember, they're watching you.

1. BEGIN WITH THE RIGHT LEADERSHIP
2. SHARE THE WHY BEFORE THE HOW
3. OPEN THE BOOKS & TEACH THE NUMBERS
4. FOCUS ON THE CRITICAL NUMBER
5. ACT ON THE RIGHT DRIVERS
6. CREATE AN EARLY WIN WITH MINIGAMES
7. PROVIDE A STAKE IN THE OUTCOME
8. KEEP SCORE
9. FOLLOW THE ACTION
10. SUSTAIN WITH HIGH-INVOLVEMENT PLANNING

STEP 10
SUSTAIN WITH HIGH-INVOLVEMENT PLANNING

People support what they help create.

igh-Involvement Planning, or HIP, has been the linchpin to SRC's sustainability of The Game and its long-term financial success. HIP has kept us focused and committed to The Game, primarily because it keeps things fresh and exciting by changing up The Game. It redefines The Game for us each year, with new Critical Numbers, new financial targets, new challenges to conquer, and new goals to achieve.

HIP is also where we leverage the business know-how we have worked so hard to create. We use this collective knowledge of our team to raise our level of thinking from ninety-day MiniGames to annual bonus plans to five- and ten-year visions for the company. The result of High-Involvement Planning is a vision and a specific plan to achieve the vision. It's also a plan that we all buy in to, believe in, and feel empowered and ready to achieve. That's a powerful position to be in. Everyone can see the big picture, which takes engagement to a whole new level and motivates the team even further. They know where we are, where we are going, how we plan to get there, and most importantly, what all that means to us and our future. That's what HIP does for SRC, and what HIP can do for you.

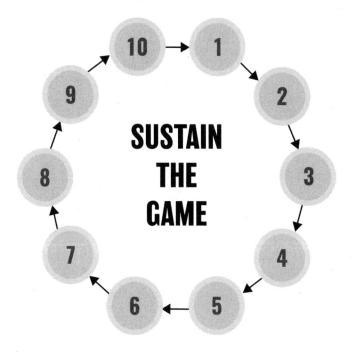

Figure 26

This chapter is designed to introduce you to the practices, steps, and tools we use to sustain The Game with High-Involvement Planning. It will take time for your Game to evolve to this level. But as it does, elevating your Game to HIP will give you the highest level of performance. Think of the first nine steps as your entry into The Game. You may spend your first year getting good at the blocking and tackling—the basics. Your first objective should be getting everyone into The Game and raising the level of understanding of the business throughout the company. Then, use HIP to leverage that knowledge and elevate and sustain The Game year after year (see figure 26). Think of HIP as the creation of a flywheel effect. It keeps The Game in motion and it continues to get stronger with each rotation. Why? Because we get smarter about our business with each rotation. We won't cover every aspect of HIP in this chapter. In fact, based on the impact HIP has had on our company (SRC), it definitely deserves its own book. However, you'll learn the core success factors that make it work, the templates that bring it to life, and tips on when and how to get started. But first, let us share with you how the practice of HIP works at SRC and the impact it has made.

USING HIP TO BUILD A $100 MILLION WAR CHEST: SRC HOLDINGS

In 2009, the world's economy ground to a halt. The mortgage industry imploded—a black swan no one saw coming—and banks stopped lending money. Everyone started chasing their deposits, and concerns grew that there would be a huge run on the banks' liquidity. But no one—not economists or government officials or financial experts—had any answers about how to stop the crisis. Then, banks and companies started closing all over the world. People were glued to the news around the clock to learn about the latest casualty. It seemed like the end of the world. Even if you had a job, you wondered if you would have one the following day. The fear was paralyzing.

The associates at SRC were scared, too—and for good reason. While the company had been through three prior recessions—it even got its start during the recession of 1983—this one was different. "Even the strongest companies were petrified," says Jack Stack, SRC's CEO. "It caught your attention. We had never seen anything like this. It came out of the blue." One of SRC's lenders had even called in its only loan of some $9 million—even though SRC had worked with them for more than twenty-five years and had $32 million deposited in the bank. The bank was trying to offer them a new deal where SRC would have to pay fees to access its own money. Rational thinking seemed to have come to an end.

The good news for SRC was that it paid off its loan and moved its money to a new bank. The company was still in relatively good shape financially—the details of which Stack laid out to his associates in a company-wide Huddle. "We wanted to stop the shock and awe," says Stack. "We wanted people to understand that we were fortunate to have a healthy balance sheet and cash in the bank. We didn't have to scramble to recover and start again. We also wanted to let them know what they needed to do to control their own destiny."

That was the day Stack stated, "Today is the day we take fear out of the organization."

Stack then laid out the company's "end of the world" scenarios—which affectionately became known to our associates as the DEFCON steps, named for the defense readiness condition steps used by the US military—to explain what would need to happen for the company to actually close its doors.

That willingness to confront the worst-case scenarios worked. The associates now understood where things stood—which helped ease their fears. When SRC conducted morale studies during this period of time, they received some of the highest scores in the company's history.

The next step was to take action. The company needed a long-term plan for how it was going to not just survive the recession but also take off when the economy finally recovered. Enter the High-Involvement Planning process.

Bring the Market to Your People

One of the strengths of SRC is that the company has always looked more to the future than the past. That's how it could fulfill its mission to protect and grow the jobs for its associates. Over its history, the company has averaged a 96 percent accuracy rate on its forward-looking five-year forecasts—which are developed through our sales and marketing planning—an important part of the HIP process.

"We are critical of ourselves all the time," says Stack. "When we talk about our planning process, we're trying to figure out what we're going to do going forward. And we do that frequently. That way we can continually adjust, learn, and get better at it. Our sales and marketing template hasn't changed for more than thirty years."

SRC's sales and marketing reviews are a part of the HIP planning rhythm that happens in June and again in October. This is where we bring the marketplace to our people. It begins with the company gathering as much macroeconomic data as it can to help assess what would happen in the marketplace over the next five and ten years. "The economy plays an important role in everything we do," says Stack. "That's where the dynamics really change. And you can break the economy down into specific pieces—the markets, where you compete. You can then bring that market data to your people, which becomes a big piece of what the forecast reveals."

Bringing the marketplace to our people also means understanding what competitors are doing and how their actions—whether that's setting prices, wage levels, or the margins they're earning—drive the action of the market. "I want our associates to understand that it's the marketplace that's setting the standards and what we need to do as a result to survive," says Stack. "It's important for people to understand that it's not the whim of leadership or a flip of the coin that determines the outcome."

Sales and marketing planning also includes finding out what a company's customers think as a way to bring the sales and marketing team together with the rest of the company. It removes the blame game and the finger-pointing between sales and production in setting up one-year and five-year forecasts that everyone believes in—which every single employee in the company gets the opportunity to vote on. That's how it becomes a plan everyone can believe in.

"HIP not only connects the dots inside the company; it teaches the associates what Game they are really in," says Stack. "It gives everyone the big picture of where we are and where we want to go."

With a forecast in place, the company can then put together the strategic plans that lay out the financial resources and people needed to reach that destination.

Another critical—and sometimes overlooked—part of the High-Involvement Planning process is contingency planning, which answers questions like the following: What if our forecasts are wrong? What happens if we lose 15 percent to 20 percent of our business overnight? What would we do? Using contingency planning tools, you set up a discipline to constantly be developing a plan B, C, and even D. "It's all about having new ideas, new products, and new markets ready in case of emergency," says Stack. "You always need to plan for the unexpected."

In 2009, SRC was forced to activate several of the contingency plans it had developed through the HIP process to help weather the economic storm and protect the jobs of its associates—which is the purpose of the forecast in the first place.

Taking Advantage of the Downturn

As the SRC team kicked off its HIP process in 2009, it began to develop an ambitious plan for the next ten years. Most companies don't try to predict recessions—they just try to react to them. SRC, on the other hand, was looking ahead to the next potential recession on the horizon—and talking about how it could take advantage of it when it came.

One of the insights SRC had learned from looking back at its experiences in prior recessions was that it had doubled in value five years after each of the three previous downturns. It did this by making investments and buying discounted businesses and properties at a time when everyone else was looking to cash out.

The other insight was that economic recessions appeared to hit in ten-year cycles. That meant that even as the company worked through the recession, staring it in the face in 2009, there would be a period of recovery followed by another downturn around 2019 or 2020. The question then became, How could the company best position itself to double in value not just by 2014 but also again in 2024? "We had learned from our experiences in the past that if you think a recession is coming, you don't want to be in debt," says Stack. "You also want to be diversified in the markets you operate in. We knew, for example, that auto parts go up in demand during recessions. And we also knew that it's good to make investments in property that's selling at a discount, especially commercial property, which can earn you cash flow by collecting rent. We also knew you could buy companies for pennies on the dollar. It's the whole theory of buying low and selling high. There's a lot to be said about buying something in a downturn."

If SRC was going to be able to take advantage of the next downturn, therefore, it was going to need to save enough money to make those kinds of investments. "When the rainy day came," says Stack, "we wanted to have the biggest umbrella in town."

The shared vision the associates arrived at through the HIP process was to save a total of $100 million over the next ten years, with the goal of investing that money in the next downturn. Since the company already had $32 million in the bank, that meant it needed to save about $7 million a year for the next decade. That goal became the long-term vision everyone in the organization could then begin to align to and play a role in achieving. "We had a plan, and now it was time to execute on it," says Stack. Even if the company's forecast about when the recession would hit was wrong, there was no downside to planning ahead to build up the health of the company's balance sheet.

That started by creating the strategies to achieve this long-term vision and Critical Number of building a $100 million war chest. Each of SRC's business units built five-year financial plans to support the vision. Annual strategic goals, including Critical Numbers, were established to move us closer each year toward achieving the vision. Company-wide scoreboards tracked progress, and many of the company's Critical Numbers and annual bonus plans were also tied to how much cash could be generated each year.

Departmental and company-wide MiniGames were run over ninety-day periods to help drive new efficiencies and generate additional savings. One example was how a corporation-wide team created a MiniGame to turn dead inventory into cash. Huddles were used to answer questions and to generate new ideas to drive the company toward its goals.

Meanwhile, the associates at SRC kept up their discipline to the High-Involvement Planning rhythm. The organization continued to revise its five-year forecasts based on market economic data while also developing contingencies in case those forecasts were wrong. It also tracked its progress toward its ten-year goal of saving $100 million. As we write this book, SRC's associates had hit their ten-year goal—a year early. And as part of its HIP process, they had begun to look ahead yet again and see what their next ten-year target might become.

"Our goal all along has been to build the long-term value of the company for our people so they can have a wonderful quality of life," says Stack. "When you plan the future out that far, and you keep checking on it every six months, it makes the present that much easier to work through. You get everyone working together. As we like to say at SRC, 'It's easy to stop one guy, but it's pretty hard to stop one hundred.' That's the beauty of the HIP process.

• • •

As this story illustrates, SRC communicated a vision but, more importantly, put a number on it. It set a goal that represented the vision that everyone could rally around ... a worthy goal.

How do you make all this happen? What's the process? How did the team at SRC work through the setting of the $100 million goal?

All these are fair questions, and in this chapter we will describe the HIP process and specifically the framework we use to create our plans, review our plans, get input and buy-in for our plans, and, of course, execute on our plans. But first, let us share with you the foundation to all our planning.

SETTING A WORTHY GOAL

The process starts with understanding The Game we are in and setting a worthy goal. Strategy is primarily an innovative, insightful answer to internal and external realities to achieve a goal. So, the first step must be establishing a worthy goal.

That's what SRC did in setting the $100 million goal. Then we tracked, measured, and forecast progress along the way to understand what strategies or adjustments to those strategies we needed to make to keep pushing toward the goal. We know the environment may change. The plan may need to be adjusted. We may not always execute like we should. But the goal remains the same. We will learn from this and adjust.

People argue that the environment is changing so quickly today that planning is no longer useful. This seems to be the next big idea. A quick search of "strategic planning is a waste of time" returns sixty-one million results. There are even a few best sellers by NextGen gurus who tout the "planning is fantasy" agenda. Perhaps they just aren't doing it right.

You still need to set goals people can get behind. You still need to align time, resources, and organizational efforts toward achieving the goal. None of that will ever change. Changing the goal just because the environment changed is often just an excuse for not achieving it. That is what we have learned at SRC, and it remains the foundation of our planning approach.

PUTTING THE HIP PROCESS IN MOTION

High-Involvement Planning consistently involves, informs, and educates the entire organization on the realities of the marketplace and the company's strategy for growth. If done right, HIP can transform planning from an annual time-consuming ritual, orchestrated from the top, into an exciting ongoing journey in which the entire organization discovers the answers to growth and success. Ultimately, it brings everyone, from the CEO to the frontline operator, into the planning process.

Let's walk you through the framework.

There are four main steps in the HIP process: create the plan, communicate the plan, commit to the plan, and execute the plan. It's a framework for setting strategy, dealing with market changes, and enabling everybody to contribute. Each step reinforces the next. They work together to bring the plan to life. This is a repeatable process that, like a flywheel, gets easier to repeat the longer you commit to keeping it in motion.

CREATE THE PLAN

First, you need the tools and templates to create the plan. The key success factor at this stage is that you need to create a plan that is first and foremost rooted in reality.

Without a consistent way of looking at the marketplace and knowing at all times what game you are in, you are kidding yourself. Remember, developing strategy is primarily an innovative, insightful answer to external (market, competitive) and internal (resources, financial) realities to achieve a goal. As a result, good plans have broad participation to provide the best possible understanding of those realities.

No More Fairy-Tale Planning

We are continually amazed by how much information we can generate about our business through the HIP process. We are also struck by how good our folks have become at presenting and articulating the reality of their businesses.

That was brought home to us several years back when a member of our board of directors made a telling comment about our planning process. He told us that in his forty-year career working for one of the largest original equipment manufacturers in our industry, he had sat through countless business-planning sessions and sales presentations—most of which he said could be described as fairy-tale planning "that always began with 'once upon a time' and ended with 'happily ever after.' But here, you guys are all about sharing reality. Whether your numbers are up or down, you understand that it's important not to sugarcoat it but to be brutally honest. And you take accountability for what you need to do differently tomorrow to change those numbers for the better. There are no fairy tales coming from this group."

Now, in this case the numbers at SRC had never been better, which leads us to joke that presentations are always great when the numbers are good. But the truth is that when we make these presentations and forecasts, we're making ourselves accountable to our peers. We know that we want to be as accurate as possible, because even if the numbers are down, people will step up to support us and turn them around.

That's the secret sauce of the HIP process—if you do it right and don't just go through the motions.

In creating our plan, we focus on four primary planning templates:

- Sales and marketing planning

- Strategy for growth planning

- Financial planning

- Succession planning

There is a reason sales is at the top of the income statement. The sales line is the determining factor for so many other decisions in the business (staffing plans, capital plans, inventory plans, product development plans, standard costs, production plans, etc.). The rest of the business plan is a natural outgrowth of the sales plan. Therefore, the first step in our planning process is the development of a believable, predictable sales line. It begins with gathering information from the marketplace in order to clearly understand the game we are in. What does the environment look like in the next year, 5 years, 10 years?

What is our plan of attack? What are our customers telling us? Who is our competition? What are our growth opportunities and potential contingencies? We have used the following template for more than 30 years to help us bring the marketplace to our people and put believability in our plan.

Sales and Marketing Planning Template

- External opportunities and threats
    - Economic, industry, market intelligence
    - Competitive intelligence
    - Customer intelligence
- Internal strengths and weaknesses
    - Financial perspective; trends/benchmarks
    - Stakeholder perspective; input survey
- Sales performance—five-year history/plan/actual/forecast
- Annual sales plan
- Growth and contingency planning
- Five-year sales outlook
- Our strategy for growth
- Buy-in

WHAT IS CONTINGENCY PLANNING?

At The Great Game of Business, we define contingency planning in business as the proactive process of planning for both the short-term and long-term security of a company. Contingency planning is sometimes known as the "Plan B," and is most often used in risk management, business continuity, and strategy.

What would you do if your company suddenly lost 10 percent of its revenue? That scenario may seem unlikely, but unexpected events and outcomes are almost a guarantee in business. So, the question becomes, "How can we use our insights and historical data to better foresee these surprises?"

Too many businesses get into trouble because they don't have well-designed contingency plans, or perhaps don't have any plans at all. Those that do have a business planning process in place often focus only on things like sales projections and ignore potential negative events that they'd rather not think about. Contingency planning is a powerful tool because it helps uncover weaknesses so that they can be proactively addressed, which ensures that a company can rally quickly when things go off course.

WHAT DOES A CONTINGENCY PLAN LOOK LIKE?

We define contingencies as products or services that have been researched, developed, and cost-justified, and are ready to be activated on very short notice. Based on this definition, consider what you would do if one of your biggest customers suddenly went out of business?

193

A contingency plan to deal with this possibility might include anticipating this risk, exploring opportunities for revenue replacement, or identifying company-wide changes that can soften the impact of a significant revenue loss.

A contingency plan works to support the broad goals and future direction of the organization. The business planning process is an integral part our open-book management structure. However, we do things a bit differently than everyone else. Our High-Involvement Planning process taps into the collective knowledge and experience of an organization by involving employees at all levels. While this may seem unnecessary or impractical, our process has been proven time and again to engage employees and produce positive results.

Contingency planning is just one component of the sales and marketing process, and it actually complements strategic and financial planning. Without a backup plan in place, all the hard work put into future plans can get derailed.

A contingency plan is typically activated when revenue drops unexpectedly. However, a plan may also be used for more positive growth situations. These might include incorporating a contingency plan into next year's sales growth plan or activating the plan in response to a sudden increase in customer demand or new market opportunities.

The process of developing contingency measures takes you out of reactive mode and puts your organization into a proactive stance. In fact, contingency planning can be a source of innovation with many of the contingency plans contributing to the ongoing growth of the business.

Once a contingency plan is activated, you must define another one to take its place. Remember, a contingency plan is a living document, and is meant to be revised or updated on at least a biannual basis.

By making contingency planning a regular part of your planning procedure, you ensure that you are always prepared to respond to crises and mitigate the damage from everything from small problems to worst-case scenarios. Once supported by your overall business planning process, a rock-solid contingency plan helps ensure growth and sustainability.

Strategy for Growth Planning Template

This planning template is focused on articulating and communicating our strategy for growth, both long term as well as short term. Some companies have a very clear understanding of where they are going, but they can't seem to execute today. Other companies are great at executing and always find a way to get it done today, but they don't really have any idea where they are going. The objective of the strategy for growth planning template is to clearly communicate the long-term vision of the company as well as the actions we need to take today to move us closer to the vision. This template bridges the short term and the long term. We use the following template, a.k.a. Playbook (figure 27), to capture and communicate our Strategy for Growth. As your can see, many of the practices of The Game that we described in earlier chapters are represented in this template. The Strategy for Growth template communicates the practices that will enable everyone to execute. Practices like Critical Numbers, bonus plans, MiniGames, Huddles, scoreboards—not to mention the continuous process of financial forecasting and reforecasting to meet your goals.

STRATEGY FOR GROWTH PLAYBOOK

LONG TERM STRATEGY		SHORT TERM STRATEGY		
10 YEAR FOCUS	5 YEAR FOCUS	1 YEAR FOCUS	3 MONTH FOCUS	WEEKLY FOCUS
SHARED PURPOSE	FINANCIAL OBJECTIVES	FINANCIAL PLAN	FINANCIAL FORECAST	STAKE IN THE OUTCOME
SHARED VISION	OBJECTIVES	GOALS	STRATEGIES & ROCKS	MEASURES
10 YEAR CRITICAL NUMBER	5 YEAR CRITICAL NUMBER	1 YEAR CRITICAL NUMBER	RIGHT DRIVERS	MINIGAMES™
SHARED VALUES	VALUE PROPOSITION	GROWTH & CONTINGENCIES	FOLLOW THE ACTION & KEEP SCORE	

Figure 27

Financial Planning Template

This planning template is focused on funding the strategy while leaving a fair return for the company. The objective of the financial planning template is to show the financial realities of the strategy. Does the strategy help us hit our financial goals? Is the strategy creating long-term value? Where are the vulnerabilities that need to be addressed? Where should we focus and invest to eliminate those vulnerabilities?

Succession Planning Template

This planning template is focused on identifying the who. Who will execute the plan? Do we have the talent and the bench strength to execute the strategy and achieve our goals?

Once you have created the plan, the next step is to communicate the plan.

COMMUNICATE THE PLAN

What's critical to the success of any planning process is the ability of the team to think strategically. This isn't an easy skill to develop. In fact, most of us only develop the skill after years of trial and error as we try to grow our businesses.

One objective of the HIP process is to accelerate this learning curve by creating a mental pattern or frequent planning rhythm for the team to use to deal with strategic issues and to sharpen its strategic thinking skills. Without this pattern, without this framework, valuable information can be overlooked or lost as employees fail to understand strategy and how it contributes to building a great company. As Jack Stack says, "Business is an unfolding drama. There are always new questions to consider, new discoveries to make, new problems to confront. To be great at business, you need to be continuously learning."

Planning rhythms accelerate learning. HIP also breaks down the traditional annual planning and budgeting process used by many companies into a *continual rhythm* that enables the organization to better respond to the changes in the market. HIP establishes a rhythm and a cadence to keep plans updated and dynamic—while also keeping people engaged and aligned with achieving those plans.

Using the planning templates described above, we establish a review process that drives the planning cycle. Although your specific planning rhythm may be different based primarily on the speed of your business, here is a good cadence to get the process started (see figure 28):

HIGH-INVOLVEMENT PLANNING RHYTHM

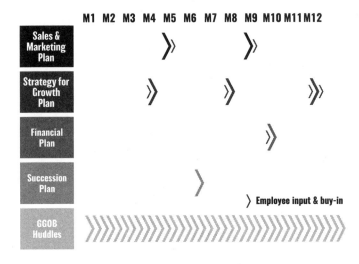

Figure 28

- Sales and marketing plan

  □ Review twice a year.

- Strategy for growth plan

  □ Review three times a year.

- Financial plan

  □ Review once a year as well as in weekly Huddles.

- Succession plan

  □ Review once a year.

- Employee input and buy-in

  □ Review three times a year as well as in weekly Huddles.

COMMIT TO THE PLAN

The way you produce the plan is just as important as the plan itself … To get ownership and ensure results, you must focus on how your plans are created and how people are involved in the process.
—Jack Stack

What makes the HIP process so effective—and why it's called *high-involvement* in the first place—is that it garners real buy-in from everyone in the organization by asking them to weigh in on how confident they are in the plan—not just the sales plan but also the contingencies and overall direction of the company. It also gives everyone a chance to provide input and hash out any weaknesses they see in it.

As you can see from the planning rhythm described above, employee input and buy-in is baked into the cycle. Think of this as closing the feedback loop. Employees are asked for their input, and then we follow up with a plan. Before it is ratified, we ask for their confidence in the plan. This allows them to see if their input was used or addressed. As part of the feedback process, employees are encouraged to make comments—which are then followed up on.

Here are example questions from both the input survey (which was explored in Step 4) and the buy-in survey:

Employee Input Survey

1. What are the top two critical *financial* issues facing the company in the next six to twelve months?

2. What are the top two critical *marketplace or customer* issues facing the company in the next six to twelve months?

3. What are the top two critical *operational or process* issues facing the company in the next six to twelve months?

4. What are the top two critical *people or culture* issues facing the company in the next six to twelve months?

5. What should the company do better, differently, or more of?

Employee Buy-In Survey

1. What is your level of confidence in our sales and marketing plan? (0 = low; 10 = high)

2. What is your level of confidence in our strategy for growth and contingency plan? (0 = low; 10 = high)

3. What was your biggest takeaway?

From our experience, it's not about what input was actually incorporated into the plan. It's about the opportunity to participate, to be listened to, and to be respected for one's thoughts and ideas. People want to be seen and heard. In the end, however, there are many times the input is heard loud and clear and reveals real issues in the plan, and that contribution builds a stronger plan.

High-Involvement Planning aims to shift everyone's mind-set from "That's *your* plan" to "This is *our* plan" by including everyone in the planning process. By now you know our mantra: *people support what they help create.* Through the years, we have learned that *if people don't participate, they don't buy in. If they don't buy in, they don't commit. If they don't commit, they don't deliver.* When people buy in and are committed to the plan (even if the plan turns out to be inadequate), they will adjust and strive to make the necessary corrections to still achieve the goal. Those who are not committed will watch, maybe even enjoy, seeing your beautiful plan crash to the ground.

Once you combine this commitment to the plan with a consistent rhythm of communicating the plan, you nearly eliminate surprises. Your people have seen the plans over and over again and have been provided the opportunity to give their feedback. You've now engaged them to help execute on the plans.

EXECUTE THE PLAN

This is where The Game comes full circle. You can now put into play all the practices of The Game to help you execute on your plans. The very plan you develop is tracked, measured, and reported week in, week out. Deviations are identified, plays are developed, and actions are taken to meet (or beat) the plan. As described in the planning cycle above, the Huddles provide the everyday review and execution of the plan. It's a powerful process to use to make sure the plans don't become stagnant or worse—not relevant.

In the end, the final High-Involvement Plan is translated into practices that will enable everyone to execute. Practices like Critical Numbers, bonus plans, MiniGames, Huddles, scoreboards, rewards, recognition, and education—not to mention the continuous process of forecasting and reforecasting to meet your goals. All these are tremendous execution practices. Best of all, they are practices used by everyone, not just the leadership team. The execution of your plan now becomes everyone's focus, and they have the tools, education, and empowerment to act.

READY, FIRE, AIM

You've read the book; you know the steps. What do you do next? Our advice is ***ready, fire, aim.*** Throughout this book, we've provided you a working knowledge of The Game, and a step by step process to implement it. You're '***ready***'. But knowing what to do isn't enough. There's a clear gap between knowing what to do and actually doing it. Now it's up to you and your people to turn these steps of implementation into action. You can't just read about it and think about it. You've got to *pull the trigger*. That's '***fire***'.

If you need to test the waters by playing a MiniGame, just don't forget that each and every one of these practices builds on the others. They support the complete system. So be careful not to approach the system piecemeal. You will certainly see early, rapid results, and of course results build momentum; but implementing the entire system is what provides sustainable, lasting change. Disciplined adherence to the system is one of the real secrets of successful GGOB companies. Staying true to the Practices, as well as the Principles, is hard work; but it's extremely rewarding. Build on your successes, learn from your mistakes, and don't give up. There will never be a perfect time to begin. It's not about perfection, it's about progress. That's '***aim***'. ***Ready, fire, aim.***

We know it's easier said than done. You may even feel a little overwhelmed with all we've shared. You might even be thinking more about all the obstacles and reasons *not* to do it than about the reasons *to* do it. Remember that you're not alone; everyone goes through this.

An AllStar Practitioner shares this advice, "Don't wait! Get started now and trust your employees. Adopt the principal of radical incrementalism. Commit to getting a little bit better each day, each week, and each year. You just need to get off the bench and get in The Game."

Get in the Game is the "How To" Implementation guide in the Great Game of Business Series. To learn more and access our Resource Site for tons of useful tools and content, visit www.greatgame.com

IT'S MONEY. IT'S PEOPLE. IT'S BOTH.

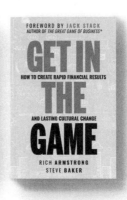

THE "WHAT"	THE "WHY"	THE "HOW"
The Origin Story of Open-Book Management	*Closing the Gap Between the Haves & Have-Nots*	*The Definitive Guide on Implementing The Great Game of Business*
The Great Game of Business started a business revolution by introducing the world to open-book management, a new way of running a business that creates unprecedented profit and employee engagement.	*Change the Game* is an inspiration, brimming with case studies of enlightened capitalism and transformed lives, proving that business is truly the catalyst for lasting change in the world. This powerful book explores the impact of business and financially literate population in every sector	*Get in the Game* is a practical guide to create rapid financial results and cultural change. It outlines the 10 Steps of Implementation with case studies from real practitioners, with all the tools, tips, and hacks that our Coaches use to implement The Game.
Paperback: $18.95 Audiobook: $19.99	Hardcover: $29.95 Audiobook: $19.99	Hardcover: $29.99 Audiobook: $19.99

HOW WE HELP

Talk with a Coach

There is no quicker, more effective way to implement The Great Game of Business than with the help of a practitioner: someone who's lived it. Our goal is to give you the tools, information and understanding necessary to be successful. To provide you with the support and extra attention you deserve, our practitioner coaches have the experience and savvy to give you the hands-on approach you're looking for and help you achieve your objectives as quickly as possible. We are happy to provide you with a complimentary thirty-minute coaching session with one of our practitioner coaches to help you start your journey. Visit www.greatgame.com to schedule today.

A PRACTITIONER'S STORY

From the very beginning our coach offered guidance that kept the implementation on track, from the right way to select the design team to working toward our critical number to the way we ran our mini-game. Without his guidance and coaching, it might have taken almost 9 months to roll out The Great Game to our team, with limited success. With his help, we kicked off our Design Team on March 1st and implemented The Great Game company-wide 113 days later. Our coach helped keep us focused, hold us accountable, and provide an objective voice in the process. For a company just launching The Great Game of Business, we would tell them to be consistent and true to The Game – consistent with huddles, consistent with weekly forecasting, consistent with reinforcing why we are playing The Game, consistent with mini-games and consistent with celebrating the wins, no matter how big or small.

Workshops, Training, and Products

For nearly forty years, people have been visiting Springfield, Missouri, to see the "Living Lab" that Jack Stack founded, in the form of SRC Holdings. Today, we continue to host numerous workshops throughout the year, both in Springfield and around the world. Learn more about our workshops, training and products at www.greatgame.com.

Attend the Annual Conference on Open-Book Management

The Gathering of Games: For nearly thirty years, the OBM Community has converged to learn, share, and celebrate the practice of The Great Game of Business. Check our website for the latest locations and schedule.

Our Committed Team

Call us. We are passionate about transforming businesses and people. We practice what we preach and are here to help. You can reach us at www.greatgame.com/getinthegame, or call 800-386-2752.

Now that you're a part of the community, you have a responsibility to engage your people, be wildly successful, and share your experience with the rest of us. We want to hear your story!

Become a Coach

If The Game has had an impact on your life, and you are ready to help others take their people and organizations to before unimagined levels of success, consider joining our Community of GGOB Coaching. Contact us at www.greatgame.com and click on "Become a Coach." Help us transform lives and change the world!

ACKNOWLEDGMENTS

We wish to our express our deep appreciation to Jack Stack, who pioneered the idea, philosophy, and practice of The Great Game of Business nearly forty years ago, transforming millions of lives in the process. Thank you for having the faith and confidence in us to share your vision.

To Bo Burlingham, who worked with Jack to write *The Great Game of Business* and *A Stake in the Outcome*. These books ignited a movement that continues to evolve and grow every day.

Special thanks to all the employee owners at SRC Holdings, who keep pushing the envelope and allowing us to share their stories from our "Living Laboratory" with the world.

Very special thanks to Ron Guinn, Krisi Schell, Rob Shear, Tim Stack, and the leadership teams at SRC of Lexington and SRC Electrical for helping us test and refine our process and for truly being our Living Lab.

To Denise Bredfeldt, the original doubter and one of the first general managers of The Great Game of Business, Inc., for her contributions to The Game.

To Tom Samsel, one of the founders of SRC, for teaching us how to coach others and mentoring us so that we could transform the lives of the people we work with.

To Donna Coppock, for her early development, documentation, and unrivaled delivery of our methodology.

To the very best work family anyone could ask for, our Great Game

Team: our veterans, Charlotte Eckley, Kristi Stringer, and Kim Brown, for sticking with us through the years; and to Ann Casstevens, Brian Underhill, Rhonda Chapman, Cassie Potts, Robbyn Pena, Cindy Laska, Donna Petiford, Dan Heisler, Lauren Haley, Chris Shelden, Michele Bridges, Darin Bridges, and Rusty Kiolbassa; and to all the past GGOB team members who helped us build our organization along the way.

To Katie Davis, who championed our Great Game for Social Sectors and Great Game for Small Business.

To Darren Dahl, without whom we could not have completed this book.

To Jack O'Riley, Kevin Walter, Dave Scholten, Wayne Whitesell, Anne-Claire Broughton, and Bill Collier, thanks for your help in contributing to and proving out our implementation approach.

To our current and past Coaches, who take The Game to the world, help organizations achieve results, and reward the people who drive those results: Doug Diamond, Bill Collier, Adam Dierselhuis, Ilan Kogus, Tom Strong, Randy Haran, Danny Clarke, Joely Anderson, Clint Hohenstein, Nicolas Hauff, Alia Stowers, Dale Meador, Michael Langhout, Chris McKittrick, Vik Karode, Natasha Nicol, Skip Weisman, Bob Washatka, Patrick Carpenter, Catherine Fitzgerald, Don Harkey, Jessica Lee and Mike Zwell. And to our Social Sector Coaches, Mark Ringenberg, Bill Griffiths, Jim O'Neal, and Tim Dobyns.

To the practitioners of The Game whose stories we've shared in this book:

Chris Sullivan, Outback Steakhouse

Kevin Walter, Tasty Catering

Liz Wilder, Anthony Wilder Design Build

Mason Ayer, Kerbey Lane Café

Ron Guinn, ReGen Technologies/SRC

Dr. David Stern, Practice Velocity

The Rolf Glass Team

Jeff Hildebrand, Hilcorp

Terry Morrill, Pacific Outdoor Living

Steve Jones, Jenner Ag

To the employee ownership community, especially Corey Rosen, Loren Rogers, and Victor Aspengren for their unfaltering support and practice of The Game.

To John Case, who wrote about the pioneers of "open-book management" and coined the term. To folks who've taken these ideas to their audiences, like Bill Fotsch and Brad Hams.

And finally, to the worldwide community of Great Game practitioners, large and small, who have applied the principles in this book, made it better, and paid it forward by teaching their people business and transforming lives every day. Thank you.

ABOUT THE AUTHORS

Rich Armstrong, President, The Great Game of Business, Inc.

Rich has nearly thirty years of experience in improving business performance and employee engagement through open-book management and employee ownership, with service as a business coach and as a current executive at SRC Holdings Corporation, a thirty-five-year-old employee-owned company and one of the United States's top one hundred largest majority employee-owned companies.

Rich has been instrumental in the ongoing development of SRC Holdings' open-book management and employee-ownership practices through practical, "firsthand" experience leading several of SRC's business units. This experience has enabled him to successfully apply these practices in both small- and large-scale company implementations around the world.

He coauthored the update to *The Great Game of Business—20th Anniversary Edition.*

Rich is a graduate of Pittsburg State University and serves on the board of the National Center for Employee Ownership (NCEO). He cherishes his time with his wife, Alicia, and four children, Ryan, Ethan, Rylee, and Jackson. Rich's guilty pleasure is making music in his home studio and playing in his '90s rock tribute band.

Steve Baker, Vice President,
The Great Game of Business, Inc.

Steve Baker is vice president of The Great Game of Business, Inc. Steve coauthored *Get in the Game* as well as the update of the number one bestseller, *The Great Game of Business—20th Anniversary Edition*. Known for his engaging and irreverent style, Steve is a top-rated, sought-after speaker and coach on open-book management, strategy and execution, leadership, and employee engagement.

His audiences range from Harvard University to the Department of Defense, and he is a regular at *Inc.* magazine's Inc. 5000 Conference. He has served on the Board of the National Center for Employee Ownership (NCEO) and SRC Holding's Ownership Culture Initiative.

Steve is an award-winning artist and lives in Springfield, Missouri, with his trophy wife, JoAnn, and three above-average children.

APPENDIX: THE HIGHER LAWS OF BUSINESS

The Great Game of Business, by Jack Stack, explains how and why we teach employees to think and act like owners. The Higher Laws of Business were introduced in 1992 in that original book. You won't find them taught in Harvard University's MBA program or in the world dictionary of business idioms. Rather, these common-sense laws exist in the minds and souls of people who are street smart and have real-life experience in the world of business. Mention any of these laws, and they'll likely grin and say, "By getting people to think at the highest level, you make it possible for them to perform up to the peak of their abilities." These rules describe the culture that is foundational to The Great Game of Business.

Higher Law #1

You Get What You Give

Employees have to understand that they have a direct role to play in creating the kind of company they want and that creating such a company is their responsibility. You spend a good portion of your waking hours at work, so why not make it more than just "screwing parts together" and punching the clock?

Higher Law #2

It's Easy to Stop One Guy, but It's Pretty Hard to Stop One Hundred

Successful businesses have employees who depend on one another and keep their promises and commitments to and with each other. The more engaged employees are in the business, the better the outcomes. If they are focused on a common goal, are armed with the knowledge to act, have the freedom to go after it, and have fire in the belly, they are unstoppable. They almost always exceed expectations.

Higher Law #3

What Goes Around, Comes Around

Lying and dishonesty have no place in business, nor does taking advantage of people or bosses acting like SOBs. We've all seen it—karma's effect as we see bad actors finally get their comeuppance. You only gain credibility by telling the truth. Business doesn't work unless employees believe you and one another. Be the kind of person you want to work for and with. Let someone else keep karma busy.

Higher Law #4

You Do What You Gotta Do

You drop everything else. You focus night and day on that one thing. You motivate, push, sneak, and threaten if needed. You do whatever it takes because people's livelihoods are on the line. Take the hill! You gotta take the hill.

Higher Law #5

You Gotta Wanna

People only get beyond work when their motivation is coming from inside. Whatever goal you are trying to accomplish, if you don't want it inside of you, it ain't gonna happen. We call it "fire in the belly." When you're a winner, nobody has to tell you. You feel it inside. You know it.

Higher Law #6

You Can Sometimes Fool the Fans, but You Can Never Fool the Players

Sometimes management forgets that workers usually know more about the products or services than they do. Rather than guess or make up answers, why not ask for help? It builds trust and credibility and shows that their opinions are valued. Besides, employees quickly figure out if you're blowing smoke, which never benefits you, them, or the company.

Higher Law #7

When You Raise the Bottom, the Top Rises

If you teach employees how their actions impact the financial numbers, they'll figure out how to improve them. Why? Because nobody wants to be on the bottom of the pile.

People want to win. They want to know they're the best at what they do, not just in the company but in the marketplace against the competition. When workers think this way, they are becoming businesspeople.

Higher Law #8

When People Set Their Own Targets, They Usually Hit Them

Our employees set their own labor and material standards, sales forecasts, and other benchmarks based on their experience and knowledge. They own those numbers for the entire year and must answer for deviations of plus or minus 5 percent from the standard. They don't set targets they can't hit. It is about keeping your word and doing what you told everyone in the company you would do.

Higher Law #9

If Nobody Pays Attention, People Stop Caring

People have to see the effects of what they do, or they won't care. It doesn't matter if the effects are good or bad. If people go to work every day and nobody acknowledges whether they are doing a good, bad, or indifferent job, they assume no one cares. Soon they stop caring too.

Higher Law #10

As They Say in Missouri, "Shit Rolls Downhill"—by Which We Mean "Change Begins at the Top"

Responsibility for the future rests squarely on the shoulders of people who run businesses. We're the only ones left with the credibility and clout to effect real change. We have to eliminate the blame game and teach people to take responsibility and become self-reliant and accountable. This won't happen unless business steps up. Since we're paying for it anyway, why not lead the charge?

The Ultimate Higher Law

When You Appeal to the Highest Level of Thinking, You Get the Highest Level of Performance

The Great Game of Business creates an environment in which you can appeal to people's best instincts, in which you ask them to rise above the day-to-day frustrations and use all their intelligence, ingenuity, and resourcefulness to help one another reach common goals. Ironically, this is also when employees are happiest and most productive.